T. N. Mic

MW00935419

Mother Mary's
ROSARIES

UDC 141.339=111=03.161.1
BBC 87.7+86.4
  M59

M59 Mickushina, T.N.

MOTHER MARY'S ROSARIES

2018. – 178 pages.

Rosaries are intended for spiritual work.

The Rosaries are composed on the basis of the Messages given by the Ascended Masters, the Teachers of mankind, through the Messenger Tatyana Nicholaevna Mickushina.

This book includes one complete Rosary – the "Rosary of Mother Mary's Mercy" compiled by T. N. Mickushina under the guidance of Mother Mary, and fourteen short Rosaries, compiled a little later, based on the inspiration of Mother Mary, and on the matrix that she gave for those people who do not have the opportunity to devote an hour to reading Rosary daily so that they can read the Rosary in short form.

UDC 141.339
BBC 87.7+86.4

Copyright © T.N. Mickushina, 2018
© Cover T.V. Martynenko
All rights reserved.

ISBN-13: 978-1727763584
ISBN-10:1727763580

Contents

Beloved, do you love me? Can you send me Love from your heart just for a few minutes before reading a Rosary every day? It is not difficult. Will you comply with my request?

I love all of you, and I will come to you while reading your Rosaries. You will feel; you will certainly feel my presence. You may stop reading and talk to me. I will lend my ear to all your requests and wishes. And I promise to render you any help that the Cosmic Law will let me render. I will do my best to help you.

Mother Mary, March 26, 2005

History of the Rosary

In Latin, the word "Rosary" means "a wreath of roses." Undoubtedly, the Blessed Virgin herself inspired different people to reading prayers.

One form of a Rosary followed another. The Rosary has been constantly modified and improved and is truly a form of people's piety. The history of Rosaries goes back centuries. It is believed that the analogue of the Rosary originated around 800, in Ireland. The monks read 150 psalms during the day, but the people who could not do this, replaced the reading of psalms with reciting the Lord's Prayer. Prayer beads were used to count the prayers.

In its infancy, the Rosary did not include the "Hail Mary" prayer. It has, as we know it today, appeared only in the 16th century. This prayer has a complicated history. Its roots lie in two texts of the Gospel of Luke: the angelic greeting ("Hail Virgin Mary, full of grace, the Lord is with thee"), and the words of Elizabeth ("Blessed art thou amongst women, and blessed is the fruit of thy womb").

After the appearance of the initial form of the "Hail Mary," in the 12th century, some Christians, began to pray, counting 150 of these prayers with beads - as well as 150 of the Lord's Prayer. These practices have gradually come together. At first, there was a Rosary of 300 prayers (150 of "The Lord's Prayer" and 150 of the "Hail Mary").

Devotees to the heart of Mary brought their prayers, the rosaries, to her like wreaths of roses. In her legendary appearance to the young monk, reciting the rosary "Hail Mary," the Blessed Virgin laid a garland of shining roses upon his shoulders. Perhaps it is since then that the prayer ritual with the use of "The Lord's prayer" and the "Hail Mary" has become known as the "Rosary."

By about 1400, some had already begun to recite the Rosary of 15 Lord's prayers and 150 Hail Mary's divided into 15 sets of 10. This Rosary used the early, short form of the "Hail Mary," and at the end of every set of 10, "Glory be to the Father ..." was not read.

At the same time, another innovation was spreading in Christian prayer: meditation on the mystery of faith, and the events of the life of Jesus and Mary. In the middle of the 15th century, one Cartesian monk made a list of 50 mysteries for contemplation followed by reading the "Hail Mary." Others also had their lists of mysteries and appropriate prayers.

8

In their modern form, the texts for contemplation are taken from Scripture, and they correspond to 15 traditional mysteries.

The practice of saying Rosaries exists in the Catholic tradition of Christianity, and has been encouraged by different Popes at different times.

The Rosary prayer, read with beads, is an alternative form of "The Lord's Prayer", the "Hail Mary," and "Glory be...", which should be accompanied by contemplation of the mysteries which correspond to certain evangelical events.

There are three sets of mysteries:

The Joyful Mysteries, in which we contemplate the mystery of God's Love:

• The Annunciation to the Virgin Mary,

• The Visitation of Virgin Mary to Elizabeth,

• The Birth of Jesus,

• The Presentation of Our Lord,

• The Finding of the Child Jesus in the Temple at Jerusalem.

The Sorrowful Mysteries, in which we contemplate the mystery of Jesus Christ, which was accomplished through His crucifixion:

• The Agony of Jesus in the Garden of Gethsemane,
• Jesus Christ is Scourged at the Pillar,

•Jesus Christ is Crowned with Thorns,
•Jesus carried the Cross,
•The Crucifixion of Our Lord.

The Glorious Mysteries, in which Jesus Christ is glorified, through whom and with whom the Christians strive for eternal life:
•The Resurrection of Jesus Christ,
•The Ascension of Jesus Christ,
•The Descent of the Holy Spirit on the Apostles,
•Assumption of the Blessed Virgin Mary,
•The Coronation of Virgin Mary as Queen of Heaven and Earth.

Every set includes 5 mysteries, so one circle of the Rosary allows us to meditate upon one set of mysteries. The complete Rosary, which includes all 3 sets of mysteries, consists, therefore, of 3 circles.

The Order of Reading the Rosary

The Rosary prayer begins by making the Sign of the Cross, followed by kissing the Crucifix on the beads, and then the introductory prayer of the Rosary is recited.

Holding the Crucifix, say the Apostles' Creed.

On the first bead, say The Lord's Prayer.

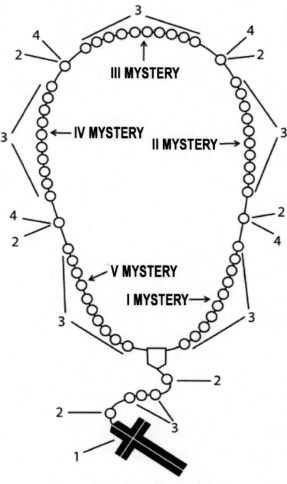

III MYSTERY

IV MYSTERY

II MYSTERY →

← V MYSTERY

I MYSTERY →

1 - Making the Sign of the Cross,
    then the Apostles' Creed
2 - The Lord's Prayer
3 - The Hail Mary
4 - Glory be to the Father

Say one "Hail Mary" on each of the next three beads. After that, say the "Glory be ...". These prayers constitute the introduction of the Rosary.

After that, the name of the set of mysteries and the first mystery are announced. On the large bead, we say "The Lord's Prayer", and on the ten smaller beads – the "Hail Mary". At the end of each mystery, we say "Glory be ...".

At the end of the Rosary prayers, the final prayers are read. In 2002, Pope St. John Paul II added (or rather, "recommended") the luminous mysteries to the three historically existing: joyful, sorrowful and glorious mysteries.

In Orthodoxy, there is no tradition of reading Rosaries. However, we can find a prototype of the prayer on beads in the Old Belief. To count prayers, the **Lestovka** was used (diminutive of old Russian "*ladder*", that is, a staircase) - a kind of prayer beads for counting prayers, a leather or cloth band sewn into a loop, and having 109 "*steps*" (also known as "*bobochki*"), divided into unequal groups.

The lestovka is closed in a ring as a sign of unceasing prayer, and at the same time it signifies the ladder of spiritual ascent from Earth to Heaven.

St. Seraphim of Sarov, who had a special relationship with the Blessed Virgin, is usually depicted with a lestovka in his hands.

Since 2000, by the great mercy of Heaven, I began hearing and distinguishing words coming from the Higher Worlds. First these were the guidelines of my Teacher, who resides in the Higher Plane of Existence. In 2004, I was granted the Mantle of the Messenger, which allows me, in a special way, at a certain time, to receive the Messages of the Masters of mankind, among whom is Beloved Mother Mary.

In 2005, based on inspiration given to me by the Teacher, I began to compose the Rosaries, in which the Catholic matrix of alternating prayers was used.

However, instead of the mysteries recited in Catholicism, the Masters recommended inserting fragments from the texts of the Messages given by them through me.

The prayer "Symbol of Creed" used by me in the Rosaries was given by my Teacher. The Lord's Prayer and the "Hail Mary" are taken from the Orthodox prayer-book.

In contrast to the usual introductory prayer ("In the name of the Father and of the Son, and of the Holy Spirit"), I also intuitively mention the

Divine Mother. And the prayer goes like this: "In the name of the Father and of the Mother and of the Son and of the Holy Spirit. Amen!"

The feminine hypostasis of the Divine - the Female, Mother aspect of God is also mentioned in the prayer "Glory be ...", that is designed to restore the disturbed balance between the male and female aspect of God's manifestation: "Glory be to the Father and to the Son, and to the Holy Spirit and to the Divine Mother as it was in the beginning, is now, and ever shall be. Amen!"

The main thing when reading Rosaries, as well as any prayers, is our complete devotion to the Will of God, the attainment of the prayerful state of consciousness that allows us to forget about ourselves, to dissolve in God.

If the Orthodox prayers "The Lord's Prayer" and the "Hail Mary" prevent your consciousness from concentrating on God, use the variant of these prayers, which is most acceptable to your consciousness.

For example, among our readers, there are a lot of people who historically profess Islam. On their initiative, and with their help and direct participation, Rosaries have been created, in which prayers from the Koran are used. For example, these two Rosaries are published in the book Rosary of the New Day-3[1] : Rosary of Truth and the Rosary "Heart."

Truly, the Rosary is a form of people's piety and it has continued to develop!

T. N. Mickushina

---

[1] Rosary of the New Day-3. / T.N. Mickushina. – Omsk: Publishing house "Sirius", 2010. – 176 p.

Rosary of Mother Mary's Mercy[2]

In the name of the Father and of the Mother
and of the Son and of the Holy Spirit.
Amen

Symbol of Creed

I believe in One God -
Creator of Heaven and Earth,
Who is present in the whole Life.
I believe in the justice of His Law
and with humility I submit to
the Wisdom of His Law.
I believe in the Kingdom of God,
manifested on Earth, as it is in Heaven.
I believe in the Oneness of God -
the Father, the Mother,
the Son and the Holy Spirit.
Amen!

---

[2] The Rosary is based on Mother Mary's dictations of December 8
and 27, 2007, as well as of January 4, July 9 and December 27,
2009.

The Lord's Prayer

Our Father, Who art in heaven!
hallowed be Thy Name;
Thy Kingdom come;
Thy will be done, on earth
as it is in heaven;
Give us this day our daily bread;
and forgive us our trespasses,
as we forgive those who
trespass against us,
and lead us not into temptation,
but deliver us from the evil one,
for Thine are the Kingdom and
the power and the glory forever.
Amen! (Matt. 6:9-13)

The Hail Mary[3] :

Hail Virgin Mary, full of grace,
the Lord is with thee.
Blessed art thou amongst women,
and blessed is the fruit of thy womb,
for thou hast borne the Saviour
of our souls (3 times).

Glory be to the Father and to the Son, and
to the Holy Spirit and to the Divine Mother
as it was in the beginning, is now,
and ever shall be.
Amen!

---

[3] In the introduction, the "Hail Mary" is recited 3 times.

I Need the Energy of Your Prayers

The Lord's Prayer[4]

1. I have come to talk to you, without any hurry... Sincerely ...Carefully, and gently. I have come as a loving and careful mother. Indeed, I am your mother for I do care about you, and heal your souls. When it is especially hard for you, all of you come to me.

The Hail Mary[5]

2. I know that it is hard for you. I know that you are at the meeting - the crossing of the new energies coming into your world and the old energies that are still prevailing in your world. It is always very hard to live at a transitional time. Your physical bodies and your more subtle conductors sometimes cannot withstand the increased load. However, you have to put up with it. There is no other way

The Hail Mary

3. Many angel-healers and many Masters are ready to give you all the feasible and possible

---

[4] Recite the Lord's Prayer once, on page 17

[5] Recite the "Hail Mary" once, on page 17

help. Therefore, do not ignore the help that the Heavens are giving to you. Turn for help to the Masters, the angels, the elementals, and to me personally.

The Hail Mary

4. I am carrying the burden of many incarnated sons and daughters of God. I am trying to ease your fate. However, you also can help me. I need your energy, your prayers, and your Love. We can and should help each other. I will ease your burden at this transitional time, and you give me an additional reserve of energy, please.

The Hail Mary

5. I am listening to your requests; and sometimes only one prayer sincerely said in your heart is enough to render help. However, you do not find time to send me the energy of your prayer. I cannot give you help when you demand help from me. I can only help humble hearts, the hearts that have repented.

The Hail Mary

6. We are calling you to the right state of your consciousness. Some people need fasting, prayer, repentance, confession, and communion in order to achieve the right state of consciousness. The

sincere tears of repentance are enough for the others. Washed by those tears, in the morning after the sleepless night, my precious children are capable of sincere prayer, and the extent of repentance present in their hearts gives me an opportunity to render the help.

The Hail Mary

7. I see your suffering. I feel compassion toward you. However, you should also understand me. There are some kinds of karma of your past deeds that can be expiated only by suffering.

The Hail Mary

8. There is a lot of grief and suffering in your world. I see it. I also see other things. I see how the young people use the precious energy of Love completely irresponsibly. I see... and my heart stops with a shudder because I know what suffering those souls will be subjected to in the future. You doom yourselves to so much suffering.

The Hail Mary

9. I have come to remind you of the responsibility for your actions so that you do not ask me for deliverance from suffering and for healing when your life is over, and you are burdened with the

heavy baggage of illnesses and psychological problems. I would like young people to ask for my help, advice, and support right now so that in their mature age, they can serve for the Glory of God and perform Divine deeds on the physical plane.

The Hail Mary

10. You all are obliged to direct your eyes at the young people. Those of you who are, at the end of life, and have finally realized the Divine Truth more or less, you can pass your experience to the new generation. Think about the way in which you can do that. It is necessary to do it, I am telling you.

The Hail Mary

Glory be to the Father and to the Son, and to the Holy Spirit and to the Divine Mother as it was in the beginning, is now, and ever shall be. Amen.

The Hour of Mercy

The Lord's Prayer

1. Every year on the 8th of December, from noon to 1 p.m. local time, you can devote your time to communicate with me. I will accept any

manifestation of your Love and gratitude. I will be with you throughout this Hour of Mercy. You can communicate with me and see me.

The Hail Mary

2. It would be as if I were beside you. I use the energy given by you in order to manifest my presence everywhere on Earth simultaneously. The purer your aspiration is, the stronger my presence beside you will be. And that is how we will be able to raise the vibrations of the physical plane every year.

The Hail Mary

3. In turn, God gives you an opportunity to ask me about manifesting your wishes concerning you or your relatives. You can ask about the manifestation of all your desires, even those that seem impossible to be realized. I will accept all your wishes in my heart and will ask God to grant your requests.

The Hail Mary

4. No matter what faith and religion you belong to, for me, you are all my children. And I will take care of you and will try to satisfy your needs and meet your requirements. You only need to give me one hour a year of your time. You can listen

to or sing songs dedicated to me; you can read Rosaries and prayers dedicated to me.

The Hail Mary

5. The impulse of your hearts, directed to me, will induce me to hear you, and I will make every effort to realize your requests. The energy of prayer and Love given by you is not always enough to realize your request. That is why I will be highly grateful to you if you can think about me more often and send me your energy of Love and prayer.

The Hail Mary

6. When a difficult situation occurs in your life, it is a signal that you haven't turned to me in a long time, and I was not able to resolve the situation and direct its course to the easiest way. Always remember that God does not want to punish you. He wants you to follow the Path of Love. If you do bad things like small children, do not forget to repent of them sincerely and ask me for help so that the mistakes you have made do not cause a severe retribution, because the Law requires that all your deeds, their energy, should be returned to you. Then you will be able to see your own mistakes and take measures to correct them.

The Hail Mary

7. No matter how many times you make mistakes, it is important that you constantly strive for righteousness and to correct the mistakes that you made. With your human consciousness you cannot estimate to what extent the things that you do are bad or good in God's eyes; therefore, ask the Heavens for help more often. Ask for the atonement of your sins.

The Hail Mary

8. Sometimes a person performs a terrible deed in the eyes of society; however, in God's eyes, this deed is not a sin because the person is being used by God as a tool so that someone can expiate his karma. That is why it is said that you do not judge. Judge not and you will not be judged. However, you should never tolerate the actions of those individuals who have forgotten themselves in play and have committed unseemly deeds expecting that God will forgive them for everything.

The Hail Mary

9. God is perfectly merciful and patient, but when a person doesn't want to learn lessons from his own behavior, then he creates a very difficult situation for himself, and according to the extent that a person can be humble under the circumstances he has gotten himself into, God judges the sincerity and repentance of the person.

The Hail Mary

10. Remember, every time you face a heavy and unfair situation in your life, from your point of view, in 100 percent of the cases, you alone were the reason for creating this situation, thanks to your wrong choices and bad deeds. Everything in your life is determined by your past choices and deeds. But there isn't any predetermination in your destiny, because sometimes one correct choice of yours and a righteous deed expiates the karma of many sins, including the most terrible ones, committed by you in the past.

The Hail Mary

Glory be to the Father and to the Son, and to the Holy Spirit and to the Divine Mother as it was in the beginning, is now, and ever shall be. Amen.

You Should Spend More Time Speaking Heart to Heart with Me

The Lord's Prayer

1. When hearts are talking, minds are silent. And true communication between us becomes possible only when we establish contact at the level of our hearts.

The Hail Mary

2. You lack for Love. You lack for Light. You are sometimes nearly out of breath due to insufficiency of Divine energy as if it were a lack of oxygen. You should spend more time speaking heart-to-heart with me.

The Hail Mary

3. I am ready to listen to all your complaints and requests. Do not feel shy. I know that men are particularly shy to show their feelings. And when a special moment of our communication comes, in confusion they brush away a tear welled up in their eyes.

The Hail Mary

4. Feel free to weep. Your soul is yearning for true communication. You are seeking for and still fail to find an ideal in your world, both men and women. You focus on your bodies, but true Love shows itself at the level of your souls and even at the level of your Higher Self.

The Hail Mary

5. Do not feel embarrassed when your eyes are misted over with tears during our communication. You committed actions that were not very good toward women, your mothers, and sisters many

times in your past lives, and during this life. May your misdeeds get dissolved in the tears, and negative energies leave you forever. Your repentance, though you may not even realize that it is repentance, opens a new opportunity for you: a new view of the world.

The Hail Mary

6. Do not feel embarrassed about your tears. They carry away the karma created by your ignorance or by your lack of wisdom. I am with you. I am always with you, and you can always turn to me for help at a hard moment of your life. I am nearer to the physical plane of planet Earth than all of the Masters. It is my special mission.

The Hail Mary

7. I guard your homes and your country. I am ready to come to you at your first call. And it all becomes possible thanks to your efforts, thanks to that energy of Love and prayer that I receive from you. The Rosaries that you dedicate to me give me an opportunity to render help for many souls seeking help.

The Hail Mary

8. I always know when you read the Rosary from the bottom of your heart. A stream of energy flows between us: an upward one from you and

a downward one from me. That is how you get my energy of Love and Mercy. When you are especially sad and you do not have any energy to read a Rosary, you can just think about me, listen to melodies dedicated to me. And then the flow of energy from you reaches me as well, and I feel you, each of you. God gave me the great mercy to feel each of His sons and daughters at the moment when they think about me, or turn to me for help. So today, you can use the opportunity granted to you by Heaven and ask me for help and support in your hour of need as before.

The Hail Mary

9. Some icons of me have a miracle-working effect. And sometimes it is enough for you just to visualize one of the icons to receive my ray of support.

The Hail Mary

10. When I have an opportunity to be present among you, and it is not a secret that God gives me such a mercy, you may not notice my presence beside you. But I am capable of being present exactly where you are. It is important for me that you are staying in the atmosphere of peace and tranquility. I come invisible and unnoticeable, and only by a slight fragrance of roses accompanying my appearance, you can occasionally guess that I have visited you.

The Hail Mary

Glory be to the Father and to the Son, and to the Holy Spirit and to the Divine Mother as it was in the beginning, is now, and ever shall be. Amen.

I Invoke Your Consciousness Heavenward

The Lord's Prayer

1. I am as close to the earthly plane as it is possible to be. Every day, I listen to all your requests and even reproaches that you send to me. I am ready to hear from you, even the not very pleasant things that you sometimes tell me. At times, in order for you to realize something, you must hear it yourselves. And when you are saying it to me, you hear it yourselves. The problems of many of your embodiments have stuck deep inside you.

The Hail Mary

2. You come up to my image and start your inner monologue. It never occurs to you that I hear every single word you are saying. And when the Divine opportunity permits, I immediately

send angels to help you. The help comes immediately in the subtle plane. And a certain time is necessary for this help to manifest itself in your physical plane.

The Hail Mary

3. But sometimes you do not wait long enough for this help to come and send me your reproaches and express your dissatisfaction. And immediately the flow of the Divine opportunity stops. And the next time you come up to my image repenting and weeping, I render my help to you again. But then everything recurs. And when you ask about one and the same thing for the fifth or seventh time, then I do not hurry to help you, because you have not realized the whole responsibility with which you burden the angelic hosts by each of your requests. Be consistent in your requests and actions.

The Hail Mary

4. Sometimes your karma does not let me intervene into your destiny, but you ask me for help every day, many times a day, for a year or even longer. And then your effort and aspiration break the invisible barrier and help flows into your being and into your life as an extensive stream.

The Hail Mary

5. Divine mercy does not know limits. The help will come from the subtle plane. Learn to use this help. Do not cut the Divine opportunity with your negative rushes. If you could keep attunement with the Divine world most of the time, how much easier it would be for us to render help to you, and how much more successfully we could progress in the transformation of the physical plane of planet Earth.

The Hail Mary

6. Every time you lose balance, you are like a small volcano. Everything around you begins shaking, and elemental life longs to move away from you because your vibrations do not let elemental beings come near you.

The Hail Mary

7. When you turn on loud music with broken rhythms, elementals and angelic beings flee headlong from the area where this awful music can be heard. The balance is disrupted to such an extent that none of the beings whose responsibility it is to restore order in the subtle plane can enter the area where the music was played for a few days. Since you turn on music every day, your towns and settlements are like deserts now because all the inhabitants of the subtle world have left these deserts and cannot help you.

The Hail Mary

8. We help you mostly through the elemental kingdom, through the elements of air, fire, water, and earth. With your behavior you deprive us of an opportunity to give you a helping hand. We need to have a harmonious atmosphere in the physical plane. And in those places on Earth where an atmosphere of peace and balance still reigns, you are healed even when you simply get into such places. Thousands of beings of elemental life are ready to render healing and help to you.

The Hail Mary

9. So think — hasn't the time come already to return to the harmony between all the kingdoms of nature that reigned in days gone by when people were happy and felt the joy of simply being? At that time, they saw elemental life and angels, and this was as natural as it is now for you to see dogs, cats, and birds. I invoke your consciousness Heavenward. I am trying to bring home to your consciousness the fact that you live in a cage and that you have encaged yourselves with your own hands and have put this cage in the desert of your cities.

The Hail Mary

10. The time is ripe to reconsider the whole system of values, and all the relationships in all

the spheres of life. How is it possible to convey to your consciousness that you live in conditions which are unworthy of a human being? Be brave to give up your affection to "the blessings" of your civilization, and you will gain genuine blessings and lasting values. Nature abhors a vacuum, and each of your negative qualities will be replaced by a Divine one, and your human attachments will be replaced by a state of Divine peace, harmony, tranquility, happiness, and joy. And this is exactly what you lack in your lives.

The Hail Mary

Glory be to the Father and to the Son, and to the Holy Spirit and to the Divine Mother as it was in the beginning, is now, and ever shall be. Amen.

Manifestation of Faith and Piety is Necessary Everywhere

The Lord's Prayer

1. You should take care not only of your physical body but also of your souls. Complaints and moans fill the space around Earth. Souls are suffering. I know that many souls are suffering,

but simultaneously with this suffering, they are purified. When a soul is alive, there is hope that a human will live.

The Hail Mary

2. Your souls need help. And I am not the only one who can give that help to your souls. You also can help yourselves. The best remedy for your souls will be sincere repentance for all the mistakes and sins that you have committed and a strong desire not to repeat those mistakes in the future. Prayer, even prayer without words, as reconciliation with the Divine world, is capable of healing many wounds of the soul.

The Hail Mary

3. I know many people who are embarrassed to pray; they hesitate to show their feelings. Beloved, my son Jesus taught not to pray in public for show, but at difficult moments, He turned to God for help Himself. You should do the same thing.

The Hail Mary

4. Consonance with the Divine world, even for a short period of time during the day, allows your soul to taste the food that is so necessary for it. Your soul is nourished on Divine grace, and you are obliged to pay attention to your soul. Not so much time is needed for that, beloved.

The Hail Mary

5. What prevents you from devoting one hour per day to sincere prayer and communication with me in your heart? I know many people who are embarrassed to pray, but they listen to songs dedicated to me at home, at work, or in their cars. And they immerse in the magical world of melody and start a quiet communication with me in their hearts.

The Hail Mary

6. Many people constantly carry my image with them. And when you secretly take my image and kiss it, I have a chance to know about that moment. And I immediately manifest my presence beside you. Yes, beloved, God gave me the opportunity to manifest my presence in many places on Earth simultaneously.

The Hail Mary

7. And where people remember me and love me, there is always a special atmosphere of protection. I am a defender of space. And very few troubles happen at those places on Earth where I can be present. If you could constantly maintain the consonance with my heart, then you and your loved ones, and all the people who live near you would be protected.

The Hail Mary

8. I would like to give my special mercy to those who are in incarnation now and perform their Service quietly and unnoticeably for the benefit of the evolutions of Earth. There are few of you, but the space around you is being purified as if from ringing bells because you are capable of cleaning the space around you with your pure thoughts, selflessness, and Service. I am granting the opportunity of a special connection with me as my gift to you. For you, I am always beside you. And I will keep my presence constantly beside you. Thus, we will be able to multiply our efforts to purify the space.

The Hail Mary

9. For those who are skeptical about me and about the Teaching that other Masters and I are giving, I have to make a special deviation. Neither the Masters nor you can change anything in your country unless the doubt in your souls gives way to devotion and Faith, and you honor my servants. The manifestation of Faith and piety is necessary everywhere, in every town, and in every village. Only true Faith can open the Divine opportunity — not a show of faith that is worthless.

The Hail Mary

10. We need a universal manifestation of Faith and reverence for the Higher Law, the Divine Law. You will know when that happens, because everything will start changing very quickly — literally in front of your eyes. Now I can only rely on a few who carry on their Service, being misunderstood and even being the mockery of their encirclement. Woe to the nation that does not respect the manifestation of true Faith and does not honor their saints. However, hope will never leave humankind while there are at least a few saints capable of maintaining the Divine level of consciousness.

The Hail Mary

Glory be to the Father and to the Son, and to the Holy Spirit and to the Divine Mother as it was in the beginning, is now, and ever shall be. Amen.

**In the name of the Father and of the Mother and of the Son and of the Holy Spirit.
Amen!**

Short Mother Mary's Rosaries

A few days after I compiled the Rosary of Mother Mary's Mercy, I woke up in the morning and felt the presence of Mother Mary. She said that it is necessary to compile short Rosaries so that people who do not have the opportunity to devote an hour to reading Rosary daily can read the Rosary in short form. She gave the matrix of the short Rosary and it is on this basis which they are composed.

Each short Mother Mary's Rosary has at its core one of the Messages that she has given through me. The first five Rosaries are included as components in the Rosary of Mother Mary's Mercy. Eight more Rosaries are compiled under the guidance of Mother Mary. In total, there are 13 short Rosaries, which can be read daily.

Mother Mary also asked to make an audio recording of all the Rosaries. She said that playing the Rosary recordings through audio equipment also cleans the space like reading Rosaries.

T.N. Mickushina

First Rosary

I Need the Energy of Your Prayers[6]

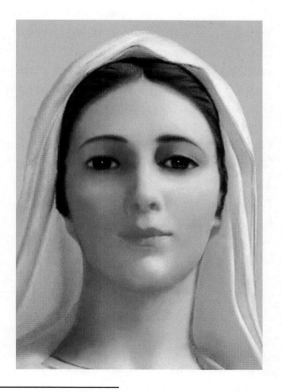

<hr>

[6] The Rosary is based on Mother Mary's dictation of December 27, 2007

In the name of I AM THAT I AM
Most Holy Mother of God,
beloved Mother Mary,
I pray on bended knee to you.
Words fail me to express the depth of
Love in my heart that I feel toward you.
Please accept my Love and gratitude.
You know what is most important for
the growth of my soul at present.
I am asking for your help and support.
I ask you to help me not to forget in
the midst of the hustle of the day
about those quiet minutes of our
commune which my soul remembers.
May my unbreakable bond with you
support me in my life and help me
not to forget about the Higher Path that
I intend to follow in this life.
Amen.[7]

In the name of the Father and of the Mother
and of the Son and of the Holy Spirit.
Amen.

---

[7] The text of the prayer to Mother Mary is translated in accordance
with the prayer given by Mother Mary in Her dictation of January
4, 2009. The book: Words of Wisdom. Messages of the Ascended
Masters, in five volumes / T. N. Mickushina. – Volume 3, 2017,
page 232.

1. I have come to talk to you, without any hurry... Sincerely ...Carefully, and gently. I have come as a loving and careful mother. Indeed, I am your mother for I do care about you, and heal your souls. When it is especially hard for you, all of you come to me.

The Hail Mary:

Hail Virgin Mary, full of grace,
the Lord is with thee.
Blessed art thou amongst women,
and blessed is the fruit of thy womb,
for thou hast borne the Saviour
of our souls.

2. I know that it is hard for you. I know that you are at the meeting - the crossing of the new energies coming into your world and the old energies that are still prevailing in your world. It is always very hard to live at a transitional time. Your physical bodies and your more subtle conductors sometimes cannot withstand the increased load. However, you have to put up with it. There is no other way.

The Hail Mary:

Hail Virgin Mary, full of grace,
the Lord is with thee.
Blessed art thou amongst women,
and blessed is the fruit of thy womb,
for thou hast borne the Saviour
of our souls.

3. Many angel-healers and many Masters are ready to give you all the feasible and possible help. Therefore, do not ignore the help that the Heavens are giving to you. Turn for help to the Masters, the angels, the elementals, and to me personally.

The Hail Mary:

Hail Virgin Mary, full of grace,
the Lord is with thee.
Blessed art thou amongst women,
and blessed is the fruit of thy womb,
for thou hast borne the Saviour
of our souls.

4. I am carrying the burden of many incarnated sons and daughters of God. I am trying to ease your fate. However, you also can help me. I need your energy, your prayers, and your Love. We can and should help each other. I will ease your burden at this transitional time, and you give me an additional reserve of energy, please.

The Hail Mary:

Hail Virgin Mary, full of grace,
the Lord is with thee.
Blessed art thou amongst women,
and blessed is the fruit of thy womb,
for thou hast borne the Saviour
of our souls.

5. I am listening to your requests; and sometimes only one prayer sincerely said in your heart is

enough to render help. However, you do not find time to send me the energy of your prayer. I cannot give you help when you demand help from me. I can only help humble hearts, the hearts that have repented.

The Hail Mary:

Hail Virgin Mary, full of grace,
the Lord is with thee.
Blessed art thou amongst women,
and blessed is the fruit of thy womb,
for thou hast borne the Saviour
of our souls.

6. We are calling you to the right state of your consciousness. Some people need fasting, prayer, repentance, confession, and communion in order to achieve the right state of consciousness. The sincere tears of repentance are enough for the others. Washed by those tears, in the morning after the sleepless night, my precious children are capable of sincere prayer, and the extent of repentance present in their hearts gives me an opportunity to render the help.

The Hail Mary:

Hail Virgin Mary, full of grace,
the Lord is with thee.
Blessed art thou amongst women,
and blessed is the fruit of thy womb,
for thou hast borne the Saviour
of our souls.

7. I see your suffering. I feel compassion toward you. However, you should also understand me. There are some kinds of karma of your past deeds that can be expiated only by suffering.

The Hail Mary:

> Hail Virgin Mary, full of grace,
> the Lord is with thee.
> Blessed art thou amongst women,
> and blessed is the fruit of thy womb,
> for thou hast borne the Saviour
> of our souls.

8. There is a lot of grief and suffering in your world. I see it. I also see other things. I see how the young people use the precious energy of Love completely irresponsibly. I see...and my heart stops with a shudder because I know what suffering those souls will be subjected to in the future. You doom yourselves to so much suffering.

The Hail Mary:

> Hail Virgin Mary, full of grace,
> the Lord is with thee.
> Blessed art thou amongst women,
> and blessed is the fruit of thy womb,
> for thou hast borne the Saviour
> of our souls.

9. I have come to remind you of the responsibility for your actions so that you do not ask me

for deliverance from suffering and for healing when your life is over, and you are burdened with the heavy baggage of illnesses and psychological problems. I would like young people to ask for my help, advice, and support right now so that in their mature age, they can serve for the Glory of God and perform Divine deeds on the physical plane.

The Hail Mary:

Hail Virgin Mary, full of grace,
the Lord is with thee.
Blessed art thou amongst women,
and blessed is the fruit of thy womb,
for thou hast borne the Saviour
of our souls.

10. You all are obliged to direct your eyes at the young people. Those of you who are, at the end of life, and have finally realized the Divine Truth more or less, you can pass your experience to the new generation. Think about the way in which you can do that. It is necessary to do it, I am telling you.

The Hail Mary:

Hail Virgin Mary, full of grace,
the Lord is with thee.
Blessed art thou amongst women,
and blessed is the fruit of thy womb,
for thou hast borne the Saviour
of our souls.

Glory be to the Father and to the Son, and to the Holy Spirit and to the Divine Mother as it was in the beginning, is now, and ever shall be. Amen.

In the name of the Father and of the Mother and of the Son and of the Holy Spirit.
Amen!

Second Rosary

The Hour of Mercy[8]

---

[8] The Rosary is based on Mother Mary's dictation of December 8, 2007

In the name of I AM THAT I AM
Most Holy Mother of God,
beloved Mother Mary,
I pray on bended knee to you.
Words fail me to express the depth of
Love in my heart that I feel toward you.
Please accept my Love and gratitude.
You know what is most important for
the growth of my soul at present.
I am asking for your help and support.
I ask you to help me not to forget in
the midst of the hustle of the day
about those quiet minutes of our
commune which my soul remembers.
May my unbreakable bond with you
support me in my life and help me
not to forget about the Higher Path that
I intend to follow in this life.
Amen.

In the name of the Father and of the Mother
and of the Son and of the Holy Spirit.
Amen.

1. Every year on the 8th of December, from noon to 1 p.m. local time, you can devote your time to communicate with me. I will accept any manifestation of your Love and gratitude. I will be with you throughout this Hour of Mercy. You can communicate with me and see me.

The Hail Mary:

Hail Virgin Mary, full of grace,
the Lord is with thee.
Blessed art thou amongst women,
and blessed is the fruit of thy womb,
for thou hast borne the Saviour
of our souls.

2. It would be as if I were beside you. I use the energy given by you in order to manifest my presence everywhere on Earth simultaneously. The purer your aspiration is, the stronger my presence beside you will be. And that is how we will be able to raise the vibrations of the physical plane every year.

The Hail Mary:

Hail Virgin Mary, full of grace,
the Lord is with thee.
Blessed art thou amongst women,
and blessed is the fruit of thy womb,
for thou hast borne the Saviour
of our souls.

3. In turn, God gives you an opportunity to ask me about manifesting your wishes concerning you or your relatives. You can ask about the manifestation of all your desires, even those that seem impossible to be realized. I will accept all your wishes in my heart and will ask God to grant your requests.

The Hail Mary:

Hail Virgin Mary, full of grace,
the Lord is with thee.
Blessed art thou amongst women,
and blessed is the fruit of thy womb,
for thou hast borne the Saviour
of our souls.

4. No matter what faith and religion you belong to, for me, you are all my children. And I will take care of you and will try to satisfy your needs and meet your requirements. You only need to give me one hour a year of your time. You can listen to or sing songs dedicated to me; you can read Rosaries and prayers dedicated to me.

The Hail Mary:

Hail Virgin Mary, full of grace,
the Lord is with thee.
Blessed art thou amongst women,
and blessed is the fruit of thy womb,
for thou hast borne the Saviour
of our souls.

5. The impulse of your hearts, directed to me, will induce me to hear you, and I will make every effort to realize your requests. The energy of prayer and Love given by you is not always enough to realize your request. That is why I will be highly grateful to you if you can think about me more often and send me your energy of Love and prayer.

The Hail Mary:

Hail Virgin Mary, full of grace,
the Lord is with thee.
Blessed art thou amongst women,
and blessed is the fruit of thy womb,
for thou hast borne the Saviour
of our souls.

6. When a difficult situation occurs in your life, it is a signal that you haven't turned to me in a long time, and I was not able to resolve the situation and direct its course to the easiest way. Always remember that God does not want to punish you. He wants you to follow the Path of Love. If you do bad things like small children, do not forget to repent of them sincerely and ask me for help so that the mistakes you have made do not cause a severe retribution, because the Law requires that all your deeds, their energy, should be returned to you. Then you will be able to see your own mistakes and take measures to correct them.

The Hail Mary:

Hail Virgin Mary, full of grace,
the Lord is with thee.
Blessed art thou amongst women,
and blessed is the fruit of thy womb,
for thou hast borne the Saviour
of our souls.

7. No matter how many times you make mistakes, it is important that you constantly strive for righteousness and to correct the mistakes that you made. With your human consciousness you cannot estimate to what extent the things that you do are bad or good in God's eyes; therefore, ask the Heavens for help more often. Ask for the atonement of your sins.

The Hail Mary:

Hail Virgin Mary, full of grace,
the Lord is with thee.
Blessed art thou amongst women,
and blessed is the fruit of thy womb,
for thou hast borne the Saviour
of our souls.

8. Sometimes a person performs a terrible deed in the eyes of society; however, in God's eyes, this deed is not a sin because the person is being used by God as a tool so that someone can expiate his karma. That is why it is said that you do not judge. Judge not and you will not be judged. However, you should never tolerate the

actions of those individuals who have forgotten themselves in play and have committed unseemly deeds expecting that God will forgive them for everything.

The Hail Mary:

Hail Virgin Mary, full of grace,
the Lord is with thee.
Blessed art thou amongst women,
and blessed is the fruit of thy womb,
for thou hast borne the Saviour
of our souls.

9. God is perfectly merciful and patient, but when a person doesn't want to learn lessons from his own behavior, then he creates a very difficult situation for himself, and according to the extent that a person can be humble under the circumstances he has gotten himself into, God judges the sincerity and repentance of the person.

The Hail Mary:

Hail Virgin Mary, full of grace,
the Lord is with thee.
Blessed art thou amongst women,
and blessed is the fruit of thy womb,
for thou hast borne the Saviour
of our souls.

10. Remember, every time you face a heavy and unfair situation in your life, from your point of view, in 100 percent of the cases, you alone were

the reason for creating this situation, thanks to your wrong choices and bad deeds. Everything in your life is determined by your past choices and deeds. But there isn't any predetermination in your destiny, because sometimes one correct choice of yours and a righteous deed expiates the karma of many sins, including the most terrible ones, committed by you in the past.

The Hail Mary:

Hail Virgin Mary, full of grace,
the Lord is with thee.
Blessed art thou amongst women,
and blessed is the fruit of thy womb,
for thou hast borne the Saviour
of our souls.

Glory be to the Father and to the Son, and to the Holy Spirit and to the Divine Mother as it was in the beginning, is now, and ever shall be. Amen.

**In the name of the Father and of
the Mother and of the Son and of
the Holy Spirit.
Amen!**

Third Rosary

You Should Spend More Time Speaking Heart to Heart with Me[9]

[9] The Rosary is based on Mother Mary's dictation of January 4, 2009

In the name of I AM THAT I AM
Most Holy Mother of God,
beloved Mother Mary,
I pray on bended knee to you.
Words fail me to express the depth of
Love in my heart that I feel toward you.
Please accept my Love and gratitude.
You know what is most important for
the growth of my soul at present.
I am asking for your help and support.
I ask you to help me not to forget in
the midst of the hustle of the day
about those quiet minutes of our
commune which my soul remembers.
May my unbreakable bond with you
support me in my life and help me
not to forget about the Higher Path that
I intend to follow in this life.
Amen.

In the name of the Father and of the Mother
and of the Son and of the Holy Spirit.
Amen.

1. When hearts are talking, minds are silent. And true communication between us becomes possible only when we establish contact at the level of our hearts.

The Hail Mary:

Hail Virgin Mary, full of grace,
the Lord is with thee.
Blessed art thou amongst women,
and blessed is the fruit of thy womb,
for thou hast borne the Saviour
of our souls.

2. You lack for Love. You lack for Light. You are sometimes nearly out of breath due to insufficiency of Divine energy as if it were a lack of oxygen. You should spend more time speaking heart-to-heart with me.

The Hail Mary:

Hail Virgin Mary, full of grace,
the Lord is with thee.
Blessed art thou amongst women,
and blessed is the fruit of thy womb,
for thou hast borne the Saviour
of our souls.

3. I am ready to listen to all your complaints and requests. Do not feel shy. I know that men are particularly shy to show their feelings. And when a special moment of our communication comes, in confusion they brush away a tear welled up in their eyes.

The Hail Mary:

Hail Virgin Mary, full of grace,
the Lord is with thee.
Blessed art thou amongst women,
and blessed is the fruit of thy womb,
for thou hast borne the Saviour
of our souls.

4. Feel free to weep. Your soul is yearning for true communication. You are seeking for and still fail to find an ideal in your world, both men and women. You focus on your bodies, but true Love shows itself at the level of your souls and even at the level of your Higher Self.

The Hail Mary:

Hail Virgin Mary, full of grace,
the Lord is with thee.
Blessed art thou amongst women,
and blessed is the fruit of thy womb,
for thou hast borne the Saviour
of our souls.

5. Do not feel embarrassed when your eyes are misted over with tears during our communication. You committed actions that were not very good toward women, your mothers, and sisters many times in your past lives, and during this life. May your misdeeds get dissolved in the tears, and negative energies leave you forever. Your repentance, though you may not even realize that

it is repentance, opens a new opportunity for you: a new view of the world.

The Hail Mary:

Hail Virgin Mary, full of grace,
the Lord is with thee.
Blessed art thou amongst women,
and blessed is the fruit of thy womb,
for thou hast borne the Saviour
of our souls.

6. Do not feel embarrassed about your tears. They carry away the karma created by your ignorance or by your lack of wisdom. I am with you. I am always with you, and you can always turn to me for help at a hard moment of your life. I am nearer to the physical plane of planet Earth than all of the Masters. It is my special mission.

The Hail Mary:

Hail Virgin Mary, full of grace,
the Lord is with thee.
Blessed art thou amongst women,
and blessed is the fruit of thy womb,
for thou hast borne the Saviour
of our souls.

7. I guard your homes and your country. I am ready to come to you at your first call. And it all becomes possible thanks to your efforts, thanks to that energy of Love and prayer that I receive

from you. The Rosaries that you dedicate to me give me an opportunity to render help for many souls seeking help.

The Hail Mary:

Hail Virgin Mary, full of grace,
the Lord is with thee.
Blessed art thou amongst women,
and blessed is the fruit of thy womb,
for thou hast borne the Saviour
of our souls.

8. I always know when you read the Rosary from the bottom of your heart. A stream of energy flows between us: an upward one from you and a downward one from me. That is how you get my energy of Love and Mercy. When you are especially sad and you do not have any energy to read a Rosary, you can just think about me, listen to melodies dedicated to me. And then the flow of energy from you reaches me as well, and I feel you, each of you. God gave me the great mercy to feel each of His sons and daughters at the moment when they think about me, or turn to me for help. So today, you can use the opportunity granted to you by Heaven and ask me for help and support in your hour of need as before.

The Hail Mary:

Hail Virgin Mary, full of grace,
the Lord is with thee.

Blessed art thou amongst women,
and blessed is the fruit of thy womb,
for thou hast borne the Saviour
of our souls.

9. Some icons of me have a miracle-working
effect. And sometimes it is enough for you just
to visualize one of the icons to receive my ray of
support.

The Hail Mary:

Hail Virgin Mary, full of grace,
the Lord is with thee.
Blessed art thou amongst women,
and blessed is the fruit of thy womb,
for thou hast borne the Saviour
of our souls.

10. When I have an opportunity to be present
among you, and it is not a secret that God gives
me such a mercy, you may not notice my presence
beside you. But I am capable of being present
exactly where you are. It is important for me that
you are staying in the atmosphere of peace and
tranquility. I come invisible and unnoticeable, and
only by a slight fragrance of roses accompanying
my appearance, you can occasionally guess that
I have visited you.

The Hail Mary:

Hail Virgin Mary, full of grace,
the Lord is with thee.

Blessed art thou amongst women,
and blessed is the fruit of thy womb,
for thou hast borne the Saviour
of our souls.

Glory be to the Father and to the Son, and
to the Holy Spirit and to the Divine Mother
as it was in the beginning, is now, and ever
shall be. Amen.

**In the name of the Father and of
the Mother and of the Son and of
the Holy Spirit.
Amen!**

Fourth Rosary

I Invoke Your Consciousness Heavenward[10]

[10] The Rosary is based on Mother Mary's dictation of July 9, 2009

In the name of I AM THAT I AM
Most Holy Mother of God,
beloved Mother Mary,
I pray on bended knee to you.
Words fail me to express the depth of
Love in my heart that I feel toward you.
Please accept my Love and gratitude.
You know what is most important for
the growth of my soul at present.
I am asking for your help and support.
I ask you to help me not to forget in
the midst of the hustle of the day
about those quiet minutes of our
commune which my soul remembers.
May my unbreakable bond with you
support me in my life and help me
not to forget about the Higher Path that
I intend to follow in this life.
Amen.

In the name of the Father and of the Mother
and of the Son and of the Holy Spirit.
Amen.

1. I am as close to the earthly plane as it is possible to be. Every day, I listen to all your requests and even reproaches that you send to me. I am ready to hear from you, even the not very pleasant things that you sometimes tell me. At times, in order for you to realize something, you must hear it yourselves. And when you are saying it to me, you hear it yourselves. The problems of many of your embodiments have stuck deep inside you.

The Hail Mary:

Hail Virgin Mary, full of grace,
the Lord is with thee.
Blessed art thou amongst women,
and blessed is the fruit of thy womb,
for thou hast borne the Saviour
of our souls.

2. You come up to my image and start your inner monologue. It never occurs to you that I hear every single word you are saying. And when the Divine opportunity permits, I immediately send angels to help you. The help comes immediately in the subtle plane. And a certain time is necessary for this help to manifest itself in your physical plane.

The Hail Mary:

Hail Virgin Mary, full of grace,
the Lord is with thee.
Blessed art thou amongst women,

and blessed is the fruit of thy womb,
for thou hast borne the Saviour
of our souls.

3. But sometimes you do not wait long enough for this help to come and send me your reproaches and express your dissatisfaction. And immediately the flow of the Divine opportunity stops. And the next time you come up to my image repenting and weeping, I render my help to you again. But then everything recurs. And when you ask about one and the same thing for the fifth or seventh time, then I do not hurry to help you, because you have not realized the whole responsibility with which you burden the angelic hosts by each of your requests. Be consistent in your requests and actions.

The Hail Mary:

Hail Virgin Mary, full of grace,
the Lord is with thee.
Blessed art thou amongst women,
and blessed is the fruit of thy womb,
for thou hast borne the Saviour
of our souls.

4. Sometimes your karma does not let me intervene into your destiny, but you ask me for help every day, many times a day, for a year or even longer. And then your effort and aspiration break the invisible barrier and help flows into your being and into your life as an extensive stream.

The Hail Mary:

Hail Virgin Mary, full of grace,
the Lord is with thee.
Blessed art thou amongst women,
and blessed is the fruit of thy womb,
for thou hast borne the Saviour
of our souls.

5. Divine mercy does not know limits. The help will come from the subtle plane. Learn to use this help. Do not cut the Divine opportunity with your negative rushes. If you could keep attunement with the Divine world most of the time, how much easier it would be for us to render help to you, and how much more successfully we could progress in the transformation of the physical plane of planet Earth.

The Hail Mary:

Hail Virgin Mary, full of grace,
the Lord is with thee.
Blessed art thou amongst women,
and blessed is the fruit of thy womb,
for thou hast borne the Saviour
of our souls.

6. Every time you lose balance, you are like a small volcano. Everything around you begins shaking, and elemental life longs to move away from you because your vibrations do not let elemental beings come near you.

The Hail Mary:

Hail Virgin Mary, full of grace,
the Lord is with thee.
Blessed art thou amongst women,
and blessed is the fruit of thy womb,
for thou hast borne the Saviour
of our souls.

7. When you turn on loud music with broken rhythms, elementals and angelic beings flee headlong from the area where this awful music can be heard. The balance is disrupted to such an extent that none of the beings whose responsibility it is to restore order in the subtle plane can enter the area where the music was played for a few days. Since you turn on music every day, your towns and settlements are like deserts now because all the inhabitants of the subtle world have left these deserts and cannot help you.

The Hail Mary:

Hail Virgin Mary, full of grace,
the Lord is with thee.
Blessed art thou amongst women,
and blessed is the fruit of thy womb,
for thou hast borne the Saviour
of our souls.

8. We help you mostly through the elemental kingdom, through the elements of air, fire, water,

and earth. With your behavior you deprive us of an opportunity to give you a helping hand. We need to have a harmonious atmosphere in the physical plane. And in those places on Earth where an atmosphere of peace and balance still reigns, you are healed even when you simply get into such places. Thousands of beings of elemental life are ready to render healing and help to you.

The Hail Mary:

Hail Virgin Mary, full of grace,
the Lord is with thee.
Blessed art thou amongst women,
and blessed is the fruit of thy womb,
for thou hast borne the Saviour
of our souls.

9. So think — hasn't the time come already to return to the harmony between all the kingdoms of nature that reigned in days gone by when people were happy and felt the joy of simply being? At that time, they saw elemental life and angels, and this was as natural as it is now for you to see dogs, cats, and birds. I invoke your consciousness Heavenward. I am trying to bring home to your consciousness the fact that you live in a cage and that you have encaged yourselves with your own hands and have put this cage in the desert of your cities.

The Hail Mary:

Hail Virgin Mary, full of grace,
the Lord is with thee.
Blessed art thou amongst women,
and blessed is the fruit of thy womb,
for thou hast borne the Saviour
of our souls.

10. The time is ripe to reconsider the whole system of values, and all the relationships in all the spheres of life. How is it possible to convey to your consciousness that you live in conditions which are unworthy of a human being? Be brave to give up your affection to "the blessings" of your civilization, and you will gain genuine blessings and lasting values. Nature abhors a vacuum, and each of your negative qualities will be replaced by a Divine one, and your human attachments will be replaced by a state of Divine peace, harmony, tranquility, happiness, and joy. And this is exactly what you lack in your lives.

The Hail Mary:

Hail Virgin Mary, full of grace,
the Lord is with thee.
Blessed art thou amongst women,
and blessed is the fruit of thy womb,
for thou hast borne the Saviour
of our souls.

Glory be to the Father and to the Son, and to the Holy Spirit and to the Divine Mother as it was in the beginning, is now, and ever shall be. Amen.

**In the name of the Father and of the Mother and of the Son and of the Holy Spirit.
Amen!**

Fifth Rosary

Manifestation of Faith and Piety is Necessary Everywhere[11]

72

In the name of I AM THAT I AM
Most Holy Mother of God,
beloved Mother Mary,
I pray on bended knee to you.
Words fail me to express the depth of
Love in my heart that I feel toward you.
Please accept my Love and gratitude.
You know what is most important for
the growth of my soul at present.
I am asking for your help and support.
I ask you to help me not to forget in
the midst of the hustle of the day
about those quiet minutes of our
commune which my soul remembers.
May my unbreakable bond with you
support me in my life and help me
not to forget about the Higher Path that
I intend to follow in this life.
Amen.

In the name of the Father and of the Mother
and of the Son and of the Holy Spirit.
Amen.

1. You should take care not only of your physical body but also of your souls. Complaints and moans fill the space around Earth. Souls are suffering. I know that many souls are suffering, but simultaneously with this suffering, they are purified. When a soul is alive, there is hope that a human will live.

The Hail Mary:

Hail Virgin Mary, full of grace,
the Lord is with thee.
Blessed art thou amongst women,
and blessed is the fruit of thy womb,
for thou hast borne the Saviour
of our souls.

2. Your souls need help. And I am not the only one who can give that help to your souls. You also can help yourselves. The best remedy for your souls will be sincere repentance for all the mistakes and sins that you have committed and a strong desire not to repeat those mistakes in the future. Prayer, even prayer without words, as reconciliation with the Divine world, is capable of healing many wounds of the soul.

The Hail Mary:

Hail Virgin Mary, full of grace,
the Lord is with thee.
Blessed art thou amongst women,
and blessed is the fruit of thy womb,

for thou hast borne the Saviour
of our souls.

3. I know many people who are embarrassed to
pray; they hesitate to show their feelings. Beloved,
my son Jesus taught not to pray in public for show,
but at difficult moments, He turned to God for help
Himself. You should do the same thing.

The Hail Mary:

Hail Virgin Mary, full of grace,
the Lord is with thee.
Blessed art thou amongst women,
and blessed is the fruit of thy womb,
for thou hast borne the Saviour
of our souls.

4. Consonance with the Divine world, even for
a short period of time during the day, allows your
soul to taste the food that is so necessary for it.
Your soul is nourished on Divine grace, and you
are obliged to pay attention to your soul. Not so
much time is needed for that, beloved.

The Hail Mary:

Hail Virgin Mary, full of grace,
the Lord is with thee.
Blessed art thou amongst women,
and blessed is the fruit of thy womb,
for thou hast borne the Saviour
of our souls.

5. What prevents you from devoting one hour per day to sincere prayer and communication with me in your heart? I know many people who are embarrassed to pray, but they listen to songs dedicated to me at home, at work, or in their cars. And they immerse in the magical world of melody and start a quiet communication with me in their hearts.

The Hail Mary:

Hail Virgin Mary, full of grace,
the Lord is with thee.
Blessed art thou amongst women,
and blessed is the fruit of thy womb,
for thou hast borne the Saviour
of our souls.

6. Many people constantly carry my image with them. And when you secretly take my image and kiss it, I have a chance to know about that moment. And I immediately manifest my presence beside you. Yes, beloved, God gave me the opportunity to manifest my presence in many places on Earth simultaneously.

The Hail Mary:

Hail Virgin Mary, full of grace,
the Lord is with thee.
Blessed art thou amongst women,
and blessed is the fruit of thy womb,
for thou hast borne the Saviour
of our souls.

7. And where people remember me and love me, there is always a special atmosphere of protection. I am a defender of space. And very few troubles happen at those places on Earth where I can be present. If you could constantly maintain the consonance with my heart, then you and your loved ones, and all the people who live near you would be protected.

The Hail Mary:

Hail Virgin Mary, full of grace,
the Lord is with thee.
Blessed art thou amongst women,
and blessed is the fruit of thy womb,
for thou hast borne the Saviour
of our souls.

8. I would like to give my special mercy to those who are in incarnation now and perform their Service quietly and unnoticeably for the benefit of the evolutions of Earth. There are few of you, but the space around you is being purified as if from ringing bells because you are capable of cleaning the space around you with your pure thoughts, selflessness, and Service. I am granting the opportunity of a special connection with me as my gift to you. For you, I am always beside you. And I will keep my presence constantly beside you. Thus, we will be able to multiply our efforts to purify the space.

The Hail Mary:

Hail Virgin Mary, full of grace,
the Lord is with thee.
Blessed art thou amongst women,
and blessed is the fruit of thy womb,
for thou hast borne the Saviour
of our souls.

9. For those who are skeptical about me and about the Teaching that other Masters and I are giving, I have to make a special deviation. Neither the Masters nor you can change anything in your country unless the doubt in your souls gives way to devotion and Faith, and you honor my servants. The manifestation of Faith and piety is necessary everywhere, in every town, and in every village. Only true Faith can open the Divine opportunity — not a show of faith that is worthless.

The Hail Mary:

Hail Virgin Mary, full of grace,
the Lord is with thee.
Blessed art thou amongst women,
and blessed is the fruit of thy womb,
for thou hast borne the Saviour
of our souls.

10. We need a universal manifestation of Faith and reverence for the Higher Law, the Divine Law. You will know when that happens, because everything will start changing very quickly —

literally in front of your eyes. Now I can only rely on a few who carry on their Service, being misunderstood and even being the mockery of their encirclement. Woe to the nation that does not respect the manifestation of true Faith and does not honor their saints. However, hope will never leave humankind while there are at least a few saints capable of maintaining the Divine level of consciousness.

The Hail Mary:

Hail Virgin Mary, full of grace,
the Lord is with thee.
Blessed art thou amongst women,
and blessed is the fruit of thy womb,
for thou hast borne the Saviour
of our souls.

Glory be to the Father and to the Son, and to the Holy Spirit and to the Divine Mother as it was in the beginning, is now, and ever shall be. Amen.

**In the name of the Father and of the Mother and of the Son and of the Holy Spirit.
Amen!**

Sixth Rosary

May the Reading of Rosaries Become the Immediate Task of Your Life[12]

---

[12] The Rosary is based on Mother Mary's dictation of March 26, 2005.

In the name of I AM THAT I AM
Most Holy Mother of God,
beloved Mother Mary,
I pray on bended knee to you.
Words fail me to express the depth of
Love in my heart that I feel toward you.
Please accept my Love and gratitude.
You know what is most important for
the growth of my soul at present.
I am asking for your help and support.
I ask you to help me not to forget in
the midst of the hustle of the day
about those quiet minutes of our
commune which my soul remembers.
May my unbreakable bond with you
support me in my life and help me
not to forget about the Higher Path that
I intend to follow in this life.
Amen.

In the name of the Father and of the Mother
and of the Son and of the Holy Spirit.
Amen.

1. Many times I came through many people who are incarnated on planet Earth today. I use the dispensation that was granted to me which allows me to use the energy people emanate while reading Rosaries, in order to manifest myself in the physical world. I come to many people, and I will have this opportunity until the stream of energy flowing from your hearts into my heart is exhausted. I use every opportunity to appear before those who are ready to see and hear me.

The Hail Mary:

> Hail Virgin Mary, full of grace,
> the Lord is with thee.
> Blessed art thou amongst women,
> and blessed is the fruit of thy womb,
> for thou hast borne the Saviour
> of our souls.

2. You may imagine me. I am standing right in front of you when you are reading these lines. I am standing in front of you with a bouquet of roses in my hands. I have prepared this bunch for you, my beloved. For you, who aspires and spends so many hours reading my Rosaries. Do not give up this work, I am asking you, my beloved. I understand that there are many temptations and seductions in your world that seem to you to be more important than the prayers that I ask you to read for me every day. However, if it were not the need of the hour and the need for your service, I would not have bothered you.

The Hail Mary:

Hail Virgin Mary, full of grace,
the Lord is with thee.
Blessed art thou amongst women,
and blessed is the fruit of thy womb,
for thou hast borne the Saviour
of our souls.

3. Beloved, it does not matter which Rosary you read - whether you read traditional Catholic Rosaries or Rosaries I have given through many Messengers lately. I would like you to understand that only your heart's aspiration and purity, and your wish to help the entire Life on this planet are of importance. I do not want to frighten you with any forthcoming calamities and cataclysms. It is not because they are not coming in the near future. Cataclysms are inevitable, as people stubbornly do not want to keep their eyes on Heaven and go on persisting in their aspiration to get more and more pleasures of this world. That is why the energy of your prayers is so necessary for us.

The Hail Mary:

Hail Virgin Mary, full of grace,
the Lord is with thee.
Blessed art thou amongst women,
and blessed is the fruit of thy womb,
for thou hast borne the Saviour
of our souls.

4. I assure each of you who read my Rosaries every day at this difficult time that within 100 kilometers around the place where you perform your daily service there will be no cataclysms or calamities.

The Hail Mary:

Hail Virgin Mary, full of grace,
the Lord is with thee.
Blessed art thou amongst women,
and blessed is the fruit of thy womb,
for thou hast borne the Saviour
of our souls.

5. May the reading of my Rosaries, no matter through which Messenger these Rosaries come to you, become the immediate task of your life in the near future. You must give me one Rosary every day. I am asking you. I am begging you, my beloved. To each of you who will commit to reading my Rosaries daily, I will come personally and give you a rose from my bouquet as a sign of my love to you.

The Hail Mary:

Hail Virgin Mary, full of grace,
the Lord is with thee.
Blessed art thou amongst women,
and blessed is the fruit of thy womb,
for thou hast borne the Saviour
of our souls.

6. I ask you to read my Rosaries with a feeling of the mightiest love you can feel towards your planet, towards all living creatures inhabiting this planet. And I ask you to enter your heart and to feel its warmth before reading a Rosary. Think of me. I know how hard it is for you to be incarnated on Earth at this difficult time. But remember how difficult it was for me when my son Jesus was crucified before my eyes. How do you think I felt watching his sufferings?

The Hail Mary:

Hail Virgin Mary, full of grace,
the Lord is with thee.
Blessed art thou amongst women,
and blessed is the fruit of thy womb,
for thou hast borne the Saviour
of our souls.

7. Beloved, do you love me? Can you send me Love from your hearts just for a few minutes before reading a Rosary every day? It is not difficult. Will you comply with my request, beloved?

The Hail Mary:

Hail Virgin Mary, full of grace,
the Lord is with thee.
Blessed art thou amongst women,
and blessed is the fruit of thy womb,
for thou hast borne the Saviour
of our souls.

8. I love all of you, and I will come to you while reading your Rosaries. You will feel; you will certainly feel my presence. You may stop reading and talk to me. I will lend my ear to all your requests and wishes. And I promise to render you any help that the Cosmic Law will let me render. I will do my best to help you. Can I also expect you to do what I ask you?

The Hail Mary:

Hail Virgin Mary, full of grace,
the Lord is with thee.
Blessed art thou amongst women,
and blessed is the fruit of thy womb,
for thou hast borne the Saviour
of our souls.

9. Believe me, if I did not know what I know and what is hidden from your eyes, I would never ask you to do the work that only you can do. Least of all I want you to feel fear. Do not be afraid of anything. I was among you; I was stepping on Earth, and I can assure you that each of you receives exactly as many trials in his life as he can withstand.

The Hail Mary:

Hail Virgin Mary, full of grace,
the Lord is with thee.
Blessed art thou amongst women,
and blessed is the fruit of thy womb,
for thou hast borne the Saviour
of our souls.

10. The karma created by mankind is too heavy. The redemption of this karma requires great sacrifices and sufferings. But God is merciful and He grants you the means, which enable you to soften your karma and ease your burden. Do not neglect these means, and do not neglect the opportunity granted to you.

The Hail Mary:

Hail Virgin Mary, full of grace,
the Lord is with thee.
Blessed art thou amongst women,
and blessed is the fruit of thy womb,
for thou hast borne the Saviour
of our souls.

Glory be to the Father and to the Son, and to the Holy Spirit and to the Divine Mother as it was in the beginning, is now, and ever shall be. Amen.

**In the name of the Father and of the Mother and of the Son and of the Holy Spirit.
Amen!**

Seventh Rosary

Do not interrupt your prayers[13]

---

[13] The Rosary is based on Mother Mary's dictation of June 13, 2005

In the name of I AM THAT I AM
Most Holy Mother of God,
beloved Mother Mary,
I pray on bended knee to you.
Words fail me to express the depth of
Love in my heart that I feel toward you.
Please accept my Love and gratitude.
You know what is most important for
the growth of my soul at present.
I am asking for your help and support.
I ask you to help me not to forget in
the midst of the hustle of the day
about those quiet minutes of our
commune which my soul remembers.
May my unbreakable bond with you
support me in my life and help me
not to forget about the Higher Path that
I intend to follow in this life.
Amen.

In the name of the Father and of the Mother
and of the Son and of the Holy Spirit.
Amen.

1. I thank all of you who have devoted all your free time to saying Rosaries. I promised to come and to gift you a rose. I have been literally pouring roses upon many of you. And if you could notice with the eyes of your souls what is taking place around you, you would be able to see that the whole room in which you are saying the Rosaries is literally heaped with roses.

The Hail Mary:

> Hail Virgin Mary, full of grace,
> the Lord is with thee.
> Blessed art thou amongst women,
> and blessed is the fruit of thy womb,
> for thou hast borne the Saviour
> of our souls.

2. My Love was invariably being poured upon you during your saying of the Rosaries. And I was feeling your Love. Oh, you cannot even imagine the bliss I experience while taking your Love into my heart. Your Love penetrates the veil and flows like blessed incense wrapping me. I always see clearly whose heart is sending me this Love, and I can always send my blessing to your heart, to your life-stream. Blessed be all those devoted and compassionate hearts who, amid the hustle and bustle of the day, find time to stop and give me Love and the energy of the Rosary.

The Hail Mary:

Hail Virgin Mary, full of grace,
the Lord is with thee.
Blessed art thou amongst women,
and blessed is the fruit of thy womb,
for thou hast borne the Saviour
of our souls.

3. Let us not interrupt this flow of Love and this energy exchange between our octaves. Just imagine that each of your prayers addressed to me makes the veil between our worlds thinner and thinner. There are regions on the globe where the power of your prayers has made the communication between our worlds possible to such an extent that you can even feel me touching you and sense the aroma of the roses I am heaping upon you. Beloved, do not interrupt your prayers. I need your Love and prayers as before.

The Hail Mary:

Hail Virgin Mary, full of grace,
the Lord is with thee.
Blessed art thou amongst women,
and blessed is the fruit of thy womb,
for thou hast borne the Saviour
of our souls.

4. You cannot even imagine this inexpressible miracle given to us by the Lord. With the help of

our Love we are able to eliminate all the barriers between our worlds. And there is nothing more elevated, pleasant and blessed than the communication that we can give each other. We exist on different sides of the border separating our worlds. However, the border itself is becoming thinner and thinner under the influence of the overmastering power of Love. There are no barriers for the power of Love, beloved. Love is capable of working miracles both in your world and ours. And Love is the very force capable of penetrating the veil.

The Hail Mary:

Hail Virgin Mary, full of grace,
the Lord is with thee.
Blessed art thou amongst women,
and blessed is the fruit of thy womb,
for thou hast borne the Saviour
of our souls.

5. When you have a minute to leave your bustle and go before my image, please do not think that I am somewhere far away. I hear the sincere call of your heart. I am where you are. I hear every word you say to me, no matter whether you pronounce these words aloud or just within your heart.

The Hail Mary:

Hail Virgin Mary, full of grace,
the Lord is with thee.

Blessed art thou amongst women,
and blessed is the fruit of thy womb,
for thou hast borne the Saviour
of our souls.

6. And if you bate your breath and look narrowly, you can even spot my presence next to you in the shape of a light, subtle cloud. You can also sense a dainty aroma of the roses or feel me touching you. I love watching your faces during your prayers. And sometimes I allow myself to approach you while you are saying the Rosaries and to kiss or stroke you. You, many of you, feel my touches and even try to drive me away like an annoying fly. Oh, if you only admitted in your consciousness a thought that it was not a fly but Mother Mary herself who came to kiss you. You would feel very awkward and funny.

The Hail Mary:

Hail Virgin Mary, full of grace,
the Lord is with thee.
Blessed art thou amongst women,
and blessed is the fruit of thy womb,
for thou hast borne the Saviour
of our souls.

7. Our worlds are much closer to each other than you can imagine. And even now, you can feel my presence during your prayers. There is no closer Master than me for the people of Earth. I answer literally all your requests. And I am very sorry that

at times your karma is so heavy that I cannot give you the help you ask me for. However, nothing is impossible for God. And after you have realized your past mistakes at the new level, it is possible that I will be allowed to help you.

The Hail Mary:

Hail Virgin Mary, full of grace,
the Lord is with thee.
Blessed art thou amongst women,
and blessed is the fruit of thy womb,
for thou hast borne the Saviour
of our souls.

8. I ask you not to stop the wheel of prayers. And if due to your stirring life you cannot dedicate much time to prayers, I think you can always find time and a chance, amid the bustle of the day, to cast a look at my image or an icon and give me your Love. It will take mere seconds. But if you are able to send me your Love just a few times during a day, this will substitute for the reading of Rosaries and prayers.

The Hail Mary:

Hail Virgin Mary, full of grace,
the Lord is with thee.
Blessed art thou amongst women,
and blessed is the fruit of thy womb,
for thou hast borne the Saviour
of our souls.

9. Always have my image with you. Keep my image in your handbag or in an amulet. Always remember that there in the physical world where my focus is, I can establish my presence owing to the energy of Love that you send me.

The Hail Mary:

> Hail Virgin Mary, full of grace,
> the Lord is with thee.
> Blessed art thou amongst women,
> and blessed is the fruit of thy womb,
> for thou hast borne the Saviour
> of our souls.

10. Please be patient, beloved. It is not too long to wait. Come out at dawn and feel the delightful moment when the Sun is still below the horizon, but everybody around is already anticipating this instant of the sunrise. And right now the whole world is at this point of expecting the rise of the Sun — the Sun of Faith, the Sun of Love, and the Sun of Hope. The sunrise of your consciousness is as inevitable as the rise of the Sun foreseen by your being.

The Hail Mary:

> Hail Virgin Mary, full of grace,
> the Lord is with thee.
> Blessed art thou amongst women,
> and blessed is the fruit of thy womb,
> for thou hast borne the Saviour
> of our souls.

Glory be to the Father and to the Son, and to the Holy Spirit and to the Divine Mother as it was in the beginning, is now, and ever shall be. Amen.

In the name of the Father and of the Mother and of the Son and of the Holy Spirit.
Amen!

Eighth Rosary

The Whole Mechanism of a Happy Life is Integrated within You[14]

---

[14] The Rosary is based on Mother Mary's dictation of June 11, 2010

In the name of I AM THAT I AM
Most Holy Mother of God,
beloved Mother Mary,
I pray on bended knee to you.
Words fail me to express the depth of
Love in my heart that I feel toward you.
Please accept my Love and gratitude.
You know what is most important for
the growth of my soul at present.
I am asking for your help and support.
I ask you to help me not to forget in
the midst of the hustle of the day
about those quiet minutes of our
commune which my soul remembers.
May my unbreakable bond with you
support me in my life and help me
not to forget about the Higher Path that
I intend to follow in this life.
Amen.

In the name of the Father and of the Mother
and of the Son and of the Holy Spirit.
Amen.

1. Many of you, particularly those who feel a special affinity to me and who read my Rosaries, come to my retreat during their nightly sleep, and I have the opportunity to talk with you. Although you forget our talks after you awaken, they still provide a significant support for your souls at this difficult time.

The Hail Mary:

Hail Virgin Mary, full of grace,
the Lord is with thee.
Blessed art thou amongst women,
and blessed is the fruit of thy womb,
for thou hast borne the Saviour
of our souls.

2. The souls of many of you cannot bear what is happening around you in your lives. When you come to me, you usually complain about your lives and ask me to take you back out of your embodiment. Many souls, the lightest and clearest, cannot adapt to the surrounding environment on the physical plane, and their souls remind me of roses trampled down in the dirt. And every night when I have the opportunity to meet with you, I straighten your petals and wash them with my tears.

The Hail Mary:

Hail Virgin Mary, full of grace,
the Lord is with thee.

Blessed art thou amongst women,
and blessed is the fruit of thy womb,
for thou hast borne the Saviour
of our souls.

3. I understand your condition very well. However, beloved, this is the state of the world now; the best souls feel depressed and do not wish to live, while the people who are not burdened with great virtues feel wonderful in the environment around them.

The Hail Mary:

Hail Virgin Mary, full of grace,
the Lord is with thee.
Blessed art thou amongst women,
and blessed is the fruit of thy womb,
for thou hast borne the Saviour
of our souls.

4. Beloved, your souls have taken upon themselves the heavy burden of incarnation at this difficult time on Earth. And I can only remind you of this and tell you words of comfort, and wipe away your tears. But you must continue to fulfill your mission. Each of you is very dear to my heart, and this special connection with me will always help you at the time when it seems to you that you do not have any energy or any possibility to bear the rudeness and ignorance around you.

The Hail Mary:

Hail Virgin Mary, full of grace,
the Lord is with thee.
Blessed art thou amongst women,
and blessed is the fruit of thy womb,
for thou hast borne the Saviour
of our souls.

5. In the most difficult moments of your life, find the strength to get in touch with me in your mind. Just think about me, and I will manifest my presence beside you and share your burden. And you will feel relief and will be able to go further through life, and completely fulfill your Service.

The Hail Mary:

Hail Virgin Mary, full of grace,
the Lord is with thee.
Blessed art thou amongst women,
and blessed is the fruit of thy womb,
for thou hast borne the Saviour
of our souls.

6. Your Service is to listen to the mockery from others and to bear all the rudeness that reigns around you. However, beloved, do not fall into condemnation. I, like my sister Quan Yin, teach you to show compassion for the souls of those who have fallen under the influence of illusion. The thirst for beauty, which is present in the souls of many people who cannot find beautiful models in

the outer world, leads to inner discord and results in rebellion which manifests harmful habits and is nothing more than the desire for self-destruction.

The Hail Mary:

Hail Virgin Mary, full of grace,
the Lord is with thee.
Blessed art thou amongst women,
and blessed is the fruit of thy womb,
for thou hast borne the Saviour
of our souls.

7. All of you lack love and harmony. Some time ago, you created your bad karma by your deeds, and now you are reaping the fruits of it. Beloved, if you can hear me now, if your souls respond to my words, please understand that all the heaviness that has fallen to your lot was created by you, by your wrong actions in the past. That is why I cannot help telling you about the repentance and the awareness of your past sins and wrong deeds.

The Hail Mary:

Hail Virgin Mary, full of grace,
the Lord is with thee.
Blessed art thou amongst women,
and blessed is the fruit of thy womb,
for thou hast borne the Saviour
of our souls.

8. As soon as you can accept within yourself that everything that happens to you has been created by you, you will take the only correct path; and if you firmly follow this path, then it will lead you out of the deadlock of dissatisfaction with your lives and of your unwillingness to live. You will feel the difference between the life around you and the life that God has commanded for you. You will be able to find in the surrounding life those true and beautiful things, that do exist, but you do not notice them because you constantly turn to where your mass media directs you.

The Hail Mary:

Hail Virgin Mary, full of grace,
the Lord is with thee.
Blessed art thou amongst women,
and blessed is the fruit of thy womb,
for thou hast borne the Saviour
of our souls.

9. We cannot be as loud-voiced as your mass media. Our voices are like the rustling of grass and the gentle murmur of a stream, so you have to attune your inner perception to our vibration, and then we can be closer to each other. And you will regain the joy of life and the meaning of your existence. When your being is filled with Divine energy, you are happy because the Divine energy that is filling you can raise your vibrations to the

most beautiful states available for you: joy, love, inner harmony, and peace.

The Hail Mary:

Hail Virgin Mary, full of grace,
the Lord is with thee.
Blessed art thou amongst women,
and blessed is the fruit of thy womb,
for thou hast borne the Saviour
of our souls.

10. Of course, your consonance with the Divine world is manifested within you, in your hearts. However, you have to take care that this consonance is not interrupted by the inferior manifestations of your world. I understand that it is very difficult to live in the world and not to feel its impact. When you make the choice in your hearts to keep consonance with the Divine world, you become capable of gradually changing the surrounding environment, step by step, removing one inferior manifestation after another. You need to follow our recommendations, and then, in my retreat, you will not have to shed floods of tears and complain about your life. The whole mechanism of a happy life is integrated within you. Why don't you use it?

The Hail Mary:

Hail Virgin Mary, full of grace,
the Lord is with thee.

Blessed art thou amongst women,
and blessed is the fruit of thy womb,
for thou hast borne the Saviour
of our souls.

Glory be to the Father and to the Son, and
to the Holy Spirit and to the Divine Mother
as it was in the beginning, is now, and ever
shall be. Amen.

**In the name of the Father and of
the Mother and of the Son and of
the Holy Spirit.
Amen!**

Ninth Rosary

The End of Darkness is Coming, and Only Light is Ahead of You![15]

---

[15] The Rosary is based on Mother Mary's dictation of June 25, 2012

In the name of I AM THAT I AM
Most Holy Mother of God,
beloved Mother Mary,
I pray on bended knee to you.
Words fail me to express the depth of
Love in my heart that I feel toward you.
Please accept my Love and gratitude.
You know what is most important for
the growth of my soul at present.
I am asking for your help and support.
I ask you to help me not to forget in
the midst of the hustle of the day
about those quiet minutes of our
commune which my soul remembers.
May my unbreakable bond with you
support me in my life and help me
not to forget about the Higher Path that
I intend to follow in this life.
Amen.

In the name of the Father and of the Mother
and of the Son and of the Holy Spirit.
Amen.

1. I AM Mother Mary. Today my arrival will not be as joyful as before because I am sad. And my sadness is associated with all the many manifestations of the opposing forces, that have fettered humanity and prevented them from seeing the perspective of the Divine Path. I am monitoring young people, and I am monitoring people of a mature age, and also the elderly. Each generation comes to this world for the implementation of its mission. And it is sad to watch people suffering without God, seeking, yet failing to find Him in the twilight that the planet has been immersed in now.

The Hail Mary:

Hail Virgin Mary, full of grace,
the Lord is with thee.
Blessed art thou amongst women,
and blessed is the fruit of thy womb,
for thou hast borne the Saviour
of our souls.

2. A more blissful course of evolution is attempting to come into your lives. All of you are in need of manifestations of the Divine energies, including the maternal energies of God that I am bringing to you. My hope is not dwindling and it cannot expire. And I am seeking to manifest my presence wherever it is possible. If you go to the forest, you will see me among the trees; if you go to the field, you will see me in the sky against

the clouds. If you are staring at a candle, I am with you, and you will feel my presence in the crackle of the candlewick, and in the flicker of the flame. If you are in the habit of looking at my icon or my image, then each time my presence becomes more perceptible, and more tangible as you spend more and more time meditating upon my image.

The Hail Mary:

Hail Virgin Mary, full of grace,
the Lord is with thee.
Blessed art thou amongst women,
and blessed is the fruit of thy womb,
for thou hast borne the Saviour
of our souls.

3. I am with you in your lives, and there are no barriers between us. I manifest my presence to every aspiring person, to everyone who by his or her Love is able to create a harmonious atmosphere in which I can manifest my presence. Every time you think of me and appeal to me, we get closer to each other. And our communication becomes possible despite the external unfavorable circumstances, and despite the dominance of inferior energies in your world.

The Hail Mary:

Hail Virgin Mary, full of grace,
the Lord is with thee.

Blessed art thou amongst women,
and blessed is the fruit of thy womb,
for thou hast borne the Saviour
of our souls.

4. I am with you against all odds. In this, my Service is manifested. And every time you devote time to a prayer or a prayer vigil, I am able to multiply your efforts a thousand-fold. That is how we will be able to overcome any resistance of the dark forces. And no matter how hard it is, no matter how many manifestations of darkness and chaos furiously rage in the end, I know that all my children will sooner or later be with me.

The Hail Mary:

Hail Virgin Mary, full of grace,
the Lord is with thee.
Blessed art thou amongst women,
and blessed is the fruit of thy womb,
for thou hast borne the Saviour
of our souls.

5. I clearly behold the day when each of you, my beloved children will be saved, having broken free from the captivity of darkness and illusion. I clearly behold the day when you will be able to overcome all your inferior states of consciousness, and all the consequences of your wrong choices in the past. I clearly behold the moment when the Divine Light will illuminate your faces, and this state of the Divine bliss will never leave you.

The Hail Mary:

Hail Virgin Mary, full of grace,
the Lord is with thee.
Blessed art thou amongst women,
and blessed is the fruit of thy womb,
for thou hast borne the Saviour
of our souls.

6. I am always with you in all the most difficult situations in which you may find yourselves in your lives. And now, when I have managed to give you a particle of my love and care, I want to appeal to you once again. Beloved, do not sink into despair and grief, or give way to despondency. There is a mechanism hidden within you that will enable you to find a way out of even the worst situation. A particle of God is shining within you. You should regularly find time during the day for your communication with God. You should constantly cultivate the feeling of the Divine within yourselves.

The Hail Mary:

Hail Virgin Mary, full of grace,
the Lord is with thee.
Blessed art thou amongst women,
and blessed is the fruit of thy womb,
for thou hast borne the Saviour
of our souls.

7. You don't need to force yourselves to pray. The prayerful state of consciousness is innate. And you just need to constantly remember our consonance, and our Oneness. Then, when you think of me, you are already taking a step closer to God. You should find more time during the day for your communication with God. When God is able to be constantly present near you, wherever you are — outside, at work, at home, in a store — everything will start changing around you, and your life will change its course and aim to follow the Divine Path of development.

The Hail Mary:

Hail Virgin Mary, full of grace,
the Lord is with thee.
Blessed art thou amongst women,
and blessed is the fruit of thy womb,
for thou hast borne the Saviour
of our souls.

8. Not much effort is required, beloved. I insist that you should constantly keep your consciousness in consonance with the Divine Reality. Use the whole range of means available to you: my images, Divine music, prayers, and Rosaries. Anything that can elevate your consciousness and raise it over the commotion reigning in your world, will bring you closer to the Path of Light that is waiting for you and will unfold itself before your very eyes immediately as soon as you prepare yourselves.

The Hail Mary:

Hail Virgin Mary, full of grace,
the Lord is with thee.
Blessed art thou amongst women,
and blessed is the fruit of thy womb,
for thou hast borne the Saviour
of our souls.

9. It is impossible for you to continue wandering in the dark. It is necessary to come out to the Path of Light, the Divine Path. Stop blaming other people, other countries and nations, your government, and state structures and institutions for your troubles and misfortune. Everything surrounding you corresponds to your level of consciousness. Change your consciousness, harmonize it with God, and everything in your lives will change, within the lifetime of one generation.

The Hail Mary:

Hail Virgin Mary, full of grace,
the Lord is with thee.
Blessed art thou amongst women,
and blessed is the fruit of thy womb,
for thou hast borne the Saviour
of our souls.

10. I am telling you that the Divine Light opportunity is within hailing distance, yet you do not see it. You need to illuminate the space around you with the Divine Light emanating from the innermost

depths of your being, and then you will obtain the understanding and knowledge that are necessary for you in order to come out of the darkness into the Light. I have come to you today to remind you that everything is possible with God. And your aspirations for the Common Weal and Good will be supported by all the Heavens and the energies of the coming New Age. You need not grieve and inflame the passions of despair. I am telling you that the end of darkness is coming, and only Light is ahead of you!

The Hail Mary:

Hail Virgin Mary, full of grace,
the Lord is with thee.
Blessed art thou amongst women,
and blessed is the fruit of thy womb,
for thou hast borne the Saviour
of our souls.

Glory be to the Father and to the Son, and to the Holy Spirit and to the Divine Mother as it was in the beginning, is now, and ever shall be. Amen.

In the name of the Father and of the Mother and of the Son and of the Holy Spirit.
Amen!

Tenth Rosary

Let God into your life[16]

In the name of I AM THAT I AM
Most Holy Mother of God,
beloved Mother Mary,
I pray on bended knee to you.
Words fail me to express the depth of
Love in my heart that I feel toward you.
Please accept my Love and gratitude.
You know what is most important for
the growth of my soul at present.
I am asking for your help and support.
I ask you to help me not to forget in
the midst of the hustle of the day
about those quiet minutes of our
commune which my soul remembers.
May my unbreakable bond with you
support me in my life and help me
not to forget about the Higher Path that
I intend to follow in this life.
Amen.

In the name of the Father and of the Mother
and of the Son and of the Holy Spirit.
Amen.

1. I AM Mother Mary. I have not come in order to have a quiet talk today. I am in a decisive mood and ready for a serious talk that we will be having. I would like to talk to you about your service and your obligations. Before coming into this incarnation, many of you have assumed many obligations upon yourselves related to your service for the world. Yet, by now you have forgotten what you have taken upon yourselves. And this is sorrowful. It is especially sorrowful now when the situation on the planet is still worsening, when darkness is obscuring people's eyes and making it impossible to take a deep breath and aspire toward bright and joyful energies of regeneration.

The Hail Mary:

> Hail Virgin Mary, full of grace,
> the Lord is with thee.
> Blessed art thou amongst women,
> and blessed is the fruit of thy womb,
> for thou hast borne the Saviour
> of our souls.

2. First of all, I am speaking to the people of my dear Russia. But I am also ready to talk with many of my beloved children scattered around the globe. I am happy when we combine our efforts together in a joint prayer for peace in the world. And I am sad when the rows of those involved in the prayers thin out, when momentary entrainment distracts you from the main thing: the

prayerful opposition against any negative forces and manifestations of your world. Together in our prayers we are able to change any situation in any country of the world. Together in our joint prayers we can reverse even the most difficult situation and direct it into an easy and joyous Divine flow.

The Hail Mary:

Hail Virgin Mary, full of grace,
the Lord is with thee.
Blessed art thou amongst women,
and blessed is the fruit of thy womb,
for thou hast borne the Saviour
of our souls.

3. I am ready to stay with you in your prayer. I am ready to join the people who appeal to me in their heartfelt prayers and ask for help. God gives you unprecedented opportunities. God is ready to come to every aspiring person during sincere prayer. And together with Him, I will stay with each of you. I am craving for the moment of your sincere prayer in order to come and to reinforce it. Sometimes I come to those of you who have assumed the obligations upon themselves to read my Rosaries every day. And how surprised and disappointed I am when instead of prayer you plunge into other things that seem more important for you. I come exactly at the time of your prayer in order to strengthen it, and to pray with you. I cannot find you, and this is very sad.

The Hail Mary:

Hail Virgin Mary, full of grace,
the Lord is with thee.
Blessed art thou amongst women,
and blessed is the fruit of thy womb,
for thou hast borne the Saviour
of our souls.

4. Beloved, do not upset me with your incon-sistency and laziness. Do understand that now your prayers can only save and improve the situation that has been formed in Russia and in the world. Only with your prayers can you prevent the most terrible thing. I am asking you. I am begging you. Beloved, it is not hard, is it? Even when you do not have time to read a Rosary, just simply aspire to me with all the love of your heart. I will meet your eyes and understand that you remember me, though the circumstances do not allow you to spare the time for praying that day. I will come to you the next day, and together we will contribute our prayerful efforts for the Common Good.

The Hail Mary:

Hail Virgin Mary, full of grace,
the Lord is with thee.
Blessed art thou amongst women,
and blessed is the fruit of thy womb,
for thou hast borne the Saviour
of our souls.

5. The power of our joint prayers is reinforced now as never before. And I assure you that we can prevent the most terrible consequences of any incorrect actions of people in the past and present if we oppose the negative energies with our faith and unity. Imagine a mighty prayer wheel that is rolling from one side of Earth to the other end. Imagine how the faithful voices of those who are praying merge into one loud voice. And this voice is heard everywhere on Earth.

The Hail Mary:

Hail Virgin Mary, full of grace,
the Lord is with thee.
Blessed art thou amongst women,
and blessed is the fruit of thy womb,
for thou hast borne the Saviour
of our souls.

6. Together we will be able to withstand! I am telling you that the situation is so difficult that it is hard to believe it. And the only thing that I am asking you for now is to give me the energy of your prayers so that I can allocate it according to my view. Entrust your prayerful efforts to me. Ask me for help and I will send my angels to help in those situations that seem unsolvable.

The Hail Mary:

Hail Virgin Mary, full of grace,
the Lord is with thee.

Blessed art thou amongst women,
and blessed is the fruit of thy womb,
for thou hast borne the Saviour
of our souls.

7. Imagine that my angels and I enter the walls of your government bodies. By our presence we will transform the situation and create the preponderance of the forces during any decision-making. Imagine me during any negotiations that are taking place at the government level, as if I were also sitting at the negotiating table, and I will supervise any decision-making in your world whether it concerns politics, the economy, education, health care, culture, or social welfare. Your visualizations and prayers will allow me and other Ascended Masters to be involved in decision-making at any national level. Thanks to such a simple practice we can reverse any situation and direct its settlement along the Divine Path.

The Hail Mary:

Hail Virgin Mary, full of grace,
the Lord is with thee.
Blessed art thou amongst women,
and blessed is the fruit of thy womb,
for thou hast borne the Saviour
of our souls.

8. I know that many people are now suffering from depression, and I know that the hearts of

many people are held captive by fear and hatred. Beloved, all this happens because of the lack of God's presence in your lives. The Divine energy is blocked by you yourselves, and also with the help of mass media, which immerses you into negative states of consciousness. Only the streams of Divine energy that you attract during your prayer can purify your bodies, your consciousness and subconsciousness, and forever liberate you from fear, depression, and hatred. Any imperfect state of your consciousness can be dissolved by the Divine energy that you will daily attract into your life with the help of your prayers.

The Hail Mary:

Hail Virgin Mary, full of grace,
the Lord is with thee.
Blessed art thou amongst women,
and blessed is the fruit of thy womb,
for thou hast borne the Saviour
of our souls.

9. I will stay with every one of you during your prayers. I will strengthen the influence of your prayers, and I will help you. But I cannot do anything for you unless you give me the energy of your prayers, and the energy of your love that you send to me while meditating on my image. Therefore, do not blame anyone if you experience negative states of consciousness, if troubles and misfortunes dim your eyes. God is so merciful that

one prayer or one fervent appeal can be enough to change any situation. You must manifest all your prayers and appeals only in the name of God. We will be able to change any situation! We will do it! The Divine miracle is beside you. It is ready to be manifested, but the energy of your prayers and of your positive aspirations toward happiness, Bliss, and Good is needed to manifest the miracle.

The Hail Mary:

Hail Virgin Mary, full of grace,
the Lord is with thee.
Blessed art thou amongst women,
and blessed is the fruit of thy womb,
for thou hast borne the Saviour
of our souls.

10. You get what you strive for. If every day you argue about everything, if you criticize your government, all the people around you, and God himself, then you will hardly achieve a positive result, and it is unlikely that you will ever be happy in your lives. If you are able to sustain faith and love in your hearts no matter what, if you are ready to protect yourselves and your nearest and dearest by your prayers and love, then the worst and irreparable things will go past you and your loved ones. And if from year to year, there are more and more people who accept the priority of God and His Law, then no difficulties, no calamities or

crises, can threaten your country and its people. You see God is always looking after you. Let God into your life. I AM Mother Mary.

The Hail Mary:

Hail Virgin Mary, full of grace,
the Lord is with thee.
Blessed art thou amongst women,
and blessed is the fruit of thy womb,
for thou hast borne the Saviour
of our souls.

Glory be to the Father and to the Son, and to the Holy Spirit and to the Divine Mother as it was in the beginning, is now, and ever shall be. Amen.

**In the name of the Father and of
the Mother and of the Son and of
the Holy Spirit.
Amen!**

Eleventh Rosary

You Should Apply Maximum Effort to Return God into Your Life[17]

---

[17] The Rosary is based on Mother Mary's dictation of December 24, 2013

In the name of I AM THAT I AM
Most Holy Mother of God,
beloved Mother Mary,
I pray on bended knee to you.
Words fail me to express the depth of
Love in my heart that I feel toward you.
Please accept my Love and gratitude.
You know what is most important for
the growth of my soul at present.
I am asking for your help and support.
I ask you to help me not to forget in
the midst of the hustle of the day
about those quiet minutes of our
commune which my soul remembers.
May my unbreakable bond with you
support me in my life and help me
not to forget about the Higher Path that
I intend to follow in this life.
Amen.

In the name of the Father and of the Mother
and of the Son and of the Holy Spirit.
Amen.

1. I AM Mother Mary. I have come to you today to show you the signs of a better life, and a better fate that awaits the sons and daughters of God on planet Earth. The twilight of your human consciousness will inevitably be replaced by a bright sunny day. The sun of your Divinity should illuminate your mind and all your thoughts and feelings. And this will happen, beloved. Now, the dark forces and energies are raging in your world. And each person transmitting light energy into your world is exposed to censure and even persecution. And this is very sorrowful.

The Hail Mary:

Hail Virgin Mary, full of grace,
the Lord is with thee.
Blessed art thou amongst women,
and blessed is the fruit of thy womb,
for thou hast borne the Saviour
of our souls.

2. Some time ago, my son Jesus experienced the manifestation of human hatred and hostility to the fullest extent. He devoted his life to serving others. Many incurably ill people were healed by Him with God's help. Many people came to see the miracles performed by my son Jesus. However, the more that He did for the people, the greater was the opposition that formed and grew stronger against Him and His mission. In terms of human logic, it is very difficult to explain what happened when the

frenzied crowd, which included the people healed by Jesus, furiously demanded the execution of my son. However, if we allow ourselves to rise to a higher level of consciousness, then that sorrowful event of Christ's crucifixion will become clear.

The Hail Mary:

Hail Virgin Mary, full of grace,
the Lord is with thee.
Blessed art thou amongst women,
and blessed is the fruit of thy womb,
for thou hast borne the Saviour
of our souls.

3. Jesus brought a huge amount of Light to the world, and it is not only the light of knowledge but also a huge amount of Divine energy. On the sub-conscious level, everything that was not from the Light felt an aversion to the mission of Christ. This aversion was the manifestation of the forces opposite to the Light. You know the law: For every action there is an equal and opposite counteraction. This law of the physical world is entirely applicable to the spiritual processes taking place in the world. If a person has the potential to bring the Divine Light into the illusory world, then he will face opposition from the forces that stand for the illusion. This is so, beloved. And this law still keeps working in your world.

The Hail Mary:

Hail Virgin Mary, full of grace,
the Lord is with thee.
Blessed art thou amongst women,
and blessed is the fruit of thy womb,
for thou hast borne the Saviour
of our souls.

4. By the example of Jesus Christ, many generations of Christians had the opportunity to study the work of this law. Many true followers of Christianity, the followers of the essence of the Teachings of Christ - but not of His letter still experience the pressure of the opposing forces. This confrontation in your world is inevitable and cannot stop all at once. Like everything in your world, the confrontation between the two main forces acting in the Universe cannot instantly stop. But, in the course of time, this opposition must become less destructive. In the distant future, these two forces will be balanced in their manifestation to such an extent that collaboration and cooperation will arise from this confrontation.

The Hail Mary:

Hail Virgin Mary, full of grace,
the Lord is with thee.
Blessed art thou amongst women,
and blessed is the fruit of thy womb,
for thou hast borne the Saviour
of our souls.

5. Many of you, beloved, confront each other. It happens even when you seem to follow the same spiritual path. This confrontation is explained by the imperfection of your world. Therefore, the two opposite forces manifest themselves through your beings. At this stage, this manifestation represents animosity, suspicion, and even hatred. One and the same person can fall under the influence of different forces during the same day. Beloved, all this happens because of the lack of Love in your hearts. And the lack of Love in your hearts is caused by the isolation of your world from the world of the Divine. No God, no Love. Therefore, you should apply maximum effort to return God into your life.

The Hail Mary:

Hail Virgin Mary, full of grace,
the Lord is with thee.
Blessed art thou amongst women,
and blessed is the fruit of thy womb,
for thou hast borne the Saviour
of our souls.

6. Look at everything that is around you in your world: advertisements, urban landscapes, gloomy faces on passers-by, and TV programs. Your world is not a friendly one. And by always staying in states of fear, tension, and gloom - people absorb these states from the outer world. Even the youth in their early years lose the charge of

130

optimism and joy that should be characteristic of a young person. True joys are being replaced by substitutes: the surrogates of movies, music, and drugs. True Love is being replaced by surrogate love, that has nothing in common with the great feeling of Love.

The Hail Mary:

Hail Virgin Mary, full of grace,
the Lord is with thee.
Blessed art thou amongst women,
and blessed is the fruit of thy womb,
for thou hast borne the Saviour
of our souls.

7. While staying in the non-divine external environment, it is very easy to lose your soul. Your time is very dangerous for the souls of many people who are in embodiment, and especially for the youth. This is why the other Masters and I come to you to give you an understanding of the processes taking place in your world, and to remind you that the world was not always so unfortunate, and that a bright future awaits humanity.

The Hail Mary:

Hail Virgin Mary, full of grace,
the Lord is with thee.
Blessed art thou amongst women,
and blessed is the fruit of thy womb,
for thou hast borne the Saviour
of our souls.

8. First, this future will germinate in the hearts of a few people who possess a strong Spirit and can oppose the surrounding illusion with their faith and devotion to God, and the Masters. Later, when there are more of these souls that have the Divine state of consciousness, humanity in its majority will start turning to the Light. And people having the state of consciousness that most of humanity currently have, will be considered exceptional black sheep who require unlimited Compassion and Love.

The Hail Mary:

Hail Virgin Mary, full of grace,
the Lord is with thee.
Blessed art thou amongst women,
and blessed is the fruit of thy womb,
for thou hast borne the Saviour
of our souls.

9. Only under the influence of Compassion, Mercy, and Love, can the souls of many of you stretch the spiritual folds of your garments and rise up to Life. The feat of my son Jesus was in the fact that He continued to feel Love toward the people who tortured Him and were out for His death. That is exactly why millions of Christians all over the world continue to worship the feat of my son.

The Hail Mary:

Hail Virgin Mary, full of grace,
the Lord is with thee.
Blessed art thou amongst women,
and blessed is the fruit of thy womb,
for thou hast borne the Saviour
of our souls.

10. I foresee that in the future many of those who are now reading this Message of mine will be able to respond with Love to all the traps and tricks of the illusory forces. And even in the face of death, my children can show Mercy and Compassion to the souls of those who torture them, for many people know not what they do. If they knew, they would never allow themselves to carry out many of their deeds. You can show the Path to many lost souls. Do pray for humanity to gain insight, and forgive everyone. I AM Mother Mary.

The Hail Mary:

Hail Virgin Mary, full of grace,
the Lord is with thee.
Blessed art thou amongst women,
and blessed is the fruit of thy womb,
for thou hast borne the Saviour
of our souls.

Glory be to the Father and to the Son, and to the Holy Spirit and to the Divine Mother as it was in the beginning, is now, and ever shall be. Amen.

In the name of the Father and of the Mother and of the Son and of the Holy Spirit.
Amen!

Twelfth Rosary

Always Stay in Love, and Everything will Start Changing around You[18]

---

[18] The Rosary is based on Mother Mary's dictation of December 23, 2014.

In the name of I AM THAT I AM
Most Holy Mother of God,
beloved Mother Mary,
I pray on bended knee to you.
Words fail me to express the depth of
Love in my heart that I feel toward you.
Please accept my Love and gratitude.
You know what is most important for
the growth of my soul at present.
I am asking for your help and support.
I ask you to help me not to forget in
the midst of the hustle of the day
about those quiet minutes of our
commune which my soul remembers.
May my unbreakable bond with you
support me in my life and help me
not to forget about the Higher Path that
I intend to follow in this life.
Amen.

In the name of the Father and of the Mother
and of the Son and of the Holy Spirit.
Amen.

1. I AM Mother Mary, having come to you. Today, I would like to talk to you about your needs and your necessities of the hour. Many of you turn to me for help. I can render my help to many of you. However, there are a certain number of souls who are so burdened by the unnecessary load of their past sins, that I wish I could, but I cannot render them my help. My angels and I are constantly in a state of service, and we pay special attention to your requests and appeals. I must tell you that even when our help cannot be given fully, we do everything possible in order to alleviate your suffering.

The Hail Mary:

Hail Virgin Mary, full of grace,
the Lord is with thee.
Blessed art thou amongst women,
and blessed is the fruit of thy womb,
for thou hast borne the Saviour
of our souls.

2. The tears of repentance that I often see in your eyes during our conversation tell me much more about you than your words, or even your prayers. You cannot imagine what kind of work the Ascended Hosts have to do in order to enable your souls to realize many of your sins and to repent for them. When repentance comes into your heart, your karmic burden becomes easier by half. And you can dissolve the remaining half

by your daily prayers and efforts aimed at relieving the plight of other suffering souls. Believe me, offering your help to suffering souls is invaluable in your time.

The Hail Mary:

Hail Virgin Mary, full of grace,
the Lord is with thee.
Blessed art thou amongst women,
and blessed is the fruit of thy womb,
for thou hast borne the Saviour
of our souls.

3. Many people do not even realize that they are suffering. They cannot understand this because there is nothing they can compare their state to. They are so burdened with their problems and concerns that they do not see even a glimmer of Light in the total darkness surrounding their lives. So, give a ray of hope to these souls. Open your hearts to Love, and send a small part of your Love to each suffering heart in your world. This will not be hard for you, will it? This will not be difficult for you, to warm the violent hearts of politicians, economists, government officials and commercial structures with your Love, will it? After all, you can overcome the stereotypes within yourself, and see in the most, in your opinion, malicious and ossified government and business officials, the hearts of people who just do not know Love.

The Hail Mary:

Hail Virgin Mary, full of grace,
the Lord is with thee.
Blessed art thou amongst women,
and blessed is the fruit of thy womb,
for thou hast borne the Saviour
of our souls.

4. Many people have fallen under the spell of the illusory forces. They are sleeping and having horrible dreams, and then they try to carry these dreams into their lives. This is because there is no God or His manifestation - Love, in the hearts of those people. The absence of God is exactly the thing that makes very many politicians do horrible deeds. If someone's Love could warm their hearts with even a small amount of Goodness and Light, we predict that many of the horrible consequences of their actions could be prevented, because they will change. The impulse of Divine energy can dissolve fear and aggression in the hearts of the most hardened criminals and God-haters.

The Hail Mary:

Hail Virgin Mary, full of grace,
the Lord is with thee.
Blessed art thou amongst women,
and blessed is the fruit of thy womb,
for thou hast borne the Saviour
of our souls.

5. It happens sometimes that at a particular moment, as if this person is awakening from a dream, tears of repentance appear on their cheeks. The repentant person can no longer cause harm to others, to children, or to elderly people. Therefore, make every effort to grow Love in your heart at this dark time, and send this Love to those who, in your opinion, need this Love so that the hearts of those people can change. This way we will be able to alter the future of the whole planet by our mutual efforts, no matter how sad and joyless the future may seem.

The Hail Mary:

Hail Virgin Mary, full of grace,
the Lord is with thee.
Blessed art thou amongst women,
and blessed is the fruit of thy womb,
for thou hast borne the Saviour
of our souls.

6. We can change any situation on planet Earth by our mutual efforts. I am urging you not to be lazy and work on yourself and on those imperfections that are still blocking the manifestation of Divine Love in your hearts. Think about what is preventing your hearts from manifesting Love. Think about how to dissolve the iciness of fear, aggression and lack of faith that literally fetters your hearts.

The Hail Mary:

Hail Virgin Mary, full of grace,
the Lord is with thee.
Blessed art thou amongst women,
and blessed is the fruit of thy womb,
for thou hast borne the Saviour
of our souls.

7. Think about what you can do for other people
- not only for your relatives, but also for all
those people on whom public opinion depends.
Sometimes, one person who has enough
influence in society can change public opinion to
overcome the negative tendencies in the world.

The Hail Mary:

Hail Virgin Mary, full of grace,
the Lord is with thee.
Blessed art thou amongst women,
and blessed is the fruit of thy womb,
for thou hast borne the Saviour
of our souls.

8. You must be firm in your faith, and with your
faith you will be able to bring so much Love into
your world that the hearts of many people will
change. Everything can be changed, beloved.
Everything is possible with God's help, absolutely
everything. You just need to focus all your efforts
on God, His presence in your lives, and His
guidance in all your deeds and actions. From day
to day, and every day.

The Hail Mary:

Hail Virgin Mary, full of grace,
the Lord is with thee.
Blessed art thou amongst women,
and blessed is the fruit of thy womb,
for thou hast borne the Saviour
of our souls.

9. Do not think about those who have forgotten God, who do not show the best of human qualities. Think about the Divine Love that is growing in your heart, every day. Always stay in Love, and everything will start changing around you.

The Hail Mary:

Hail Virgin Mary, full of grace,
the Lord is with thee.
Blessed art thou amongst women,
and blessed is the fruit of thy womb,
for thou hast borne the Saviour
of our souls.

10. If you lack faith and devotion - remember me. Remember those quiet moments when you were able to catch My eye looking at My image, you get an answer to your question. Remember the moments of quite joy during our direct communication that you experienced in your life, at least once in a while. Beloved, I am always with you! We are together! I share completely all your misfortune and suffering, and I do everything to

alleviate them, as much as possible. May peace, calmness, and goodness always be with you. I AM Mother Mary, loving you and taking care of you.

The Hail Mary:

Hail Virgin Mary, full of grace,
the Lord is with thee.
Blessed art thou amongst women,
and blessed is the fruit of thy womb,
for thou hast borne the Saviour
of our souls.

Glory be to the Father and to the Son, and to the Holy Spirit and to the Divine Mother as it was in the beginning, is now, and ever shall be. Amen.

**In the name of the Father and of
the Mother and of the Son and of
the Holy Spirit.
Amen!**

144

Mother Mary's Rosaries for Russia

Very soon the people of the entire world will be surprised when they hear about, and see all the changes that will be taking place in Russia. The changes in this country will not come from those in power, from politicians or economists; the changes will come from the people's hearts, and those changes will be impossible to miss.

From the Message of Mother Mary of June 25, 2007

Russia will become the country where God will be glorified the most.

From Mother Mary's prophecy in Medjugorje

Rosary for Russia

Spiritual Mission of Russia[19]

---

[19] The Rosary is based on Mother Mary's dictation of June 25, 2007

In the name of I AM THAT I AM
Most Holy Mother of God,
beloved Mother Mary,
I pray on bended knee to you.
Words fail me to express the depth of
Love in my heart that I feel toward you.
Please accept my Love and gratitude.
You know what is most important for
the growth of my soul at present.
I am asking for your help and support.
I ask you to help me not to forget in
the midst of the hustle of the day
about those quiet minutes of our
commune which my soul remembers.
May my unbreakable bond with you
support me in my life and help me
not to forget about the Higher Path that
I intend to follow in this life.
Amen.

In the name of the Father and of the Mother
and of the Son and of the Holy Spirit.
Amen.

147

1. I AM Mother Mary. I cannot wait to bring such joyous news to you! You know that I am the patron of Russia, and you also know that the people of this country have been giving their attention to me in their prayers since the oldest of times. I help to heal. My icons have miracle-working power; they protect and heal those who need to be protected and healed. I put my presence in many of my icons, and you can always obtain answers to the questions that are troubling you by looking at my facial expression and into my eyes. I strive to communicate with you and I help you as much as I can, my beloved children.

The Hail Mary:

Hail Virgin Mary, full of grace,
the Lord is with thee.
Blessed art thou amongst women,
and blessed is the fruit of thy womb,
for thou hast borne the Saviour
of our souls.

2. That joyous news that I would like to convey to you concerns my beloved Russia. You know that a great mission is in store for this country — the mission to lead people along the spiritual Path. And now the path has finally opened up, and Russia has come to a point in its path where its future mission is already visible, the point that presupposes the uncovering of this mission. You know that many prophets of the past spoke about the great role and mission of this country.

We carefully observed the development of those individuals whose fates are connected with Russia and who have been incarnating in Russia for many centuries. You know, we came to the conclusion that thanks to its best representatives, Russia has earned the right to step on the Path as the spiritual leader of the world.

The Hail Mary:

Hail Virgin Mary, full of grace,
the Lord is with thee.
Blessed art thou amongst women,
and blessed is the fruit of thy womb,
for thou hast borne the Saviour
of our souls.

3. Russia is being called upon to become a highly spiritual country. It is at this very time, despite a seeming lack of spirituality, that the foundation for this future spiritual country is being created. It is at this time that the people of Russia who are tired of despair and lack of faith, are ready to turn to the source of Divine goodness, to get down on their knees and say inside their hearts: "Lord, forgive me, Lord, forgive us, Heavenly Father. We did not know what we were doing. We relied on our flesh, and we created many woes due to our foolishness. Lord, please, answer our prayer. Forgive us, O Lord, for everything that we have done, for all the woes and misfortunes that we have brought to the world. Lord, if it be Your Will, come to our country, enlighten us, and help us follow Your Path."

The Hail Mary:

Hail Virgin Mary, full of grace,
the Lord is with thee.
Blessed art thou amongst women,
and blessed is the fruit of thy womb,
for thou hast borne the Saviour
of our souls.

4. It is only after the people of Russia, represented by its best sons and daughters, repent in their hearts that an unprecedented Divine opportunity will open up for that country. You will soon face a tremendous explosion of spirituality in Russia. It will not matter to you which temple you visit, or at which temple you kneel. That is because in your consciousness you will rise to the Divine peak from which you will no longer see the former contradictions between different faiths and religions. Your hearts will become filled with such Divine goodness that you will stop experiencing any negative reactions toward your neighbors who are different than you.

The Hail Mary:

Hail Virgin Mary, full of grace,
the Lord is with thee.
Blessed art thou amongst women,
and blessed is the fruit of thy womb,
for thou hast borne the Saviour
of our souls.

5. You should unite in the longing of your hearts. You should unite in the motto calling for spiritual unity in the nation. Only after repentance, is spiritual unity possible. And only after spiritual unity will Russia become capable of bringing to the physical plane the models of spiritual creations of the best representatives of mankind, which are now established in the subtle plane and are ready to be precipitated on to the physical plane

The Hail Mary:

Hail Virgin Mary, full of grace,
the Lord is with thee.
Blessed art thou amongst women,
and blessed is the fruit of thy womb,
for thou hast borne the Saviour
of our souls.

6. I need to tell you that the future of Russia is not related to the adherence to a certain faith, but to the tolerance of any true manifestation of the worship of God. I am not talking about the manifestations of religious intolerance that took place in the past. I am talking about a new level of consciousness of a different quality that will embrace the Divinity, and reduce all the contradictions that the cunning human mind has been purposefully intensifying over the past millennia.

The Hail Mary:

Hail Virgin Mary, full of grace,
the Lord is with thee.
Blessed art thou amongst women,
and blessed is the fruit of thy womb,
for thou hast borne the Saviour
of our souls.

7. I have come to you on this day to bring to your consciousness the need to understand the mission of Russia. I have not come for you to be proud, but for you to lift your spirits and be able to rise to the new stage of development. The dark night is over for Russia. Come outside at dawn and watch the sunrise. In the same way, the sun of the Divine consciousness has started to rise in the people of Russia.

The Hail Mary:

Hail Virgin Mary, full of grace,
the Lord is with thee.
Blessed art thou amongst women,
and blessed is the fruit of thy womb,
for thou hast borne the Saviour
of our souls.

8. Stop looking back at the West. Stop accepting models that are not only useless, but also harmful. Your mission is to bring in new models. Very soon the people of the entire world will be surprised when they hear about, and see all the changes that will be taking place in Russia. The changes

in this country will not come from those in power, from politicians or economists; the changes will come from the people's hearts, and those changes will be impossible to miss.

The Hail Mary:

Hail Virgin Mary, full of grace,
the Lord is with thee.
Blessed art thou amongst women,
and blessed is the fruit of thy womb,
for thou hast borne the Saviour
of our souls.

9. Every time you look into the eyes of those little human beings who have come into incarnation again, try to understand the message that those eyes contain. Your responsibility is not only to help the new generation to receive everything necessary on the material plane. Your task is also to provide assistance to each of the newly incarnated people to fulfill their Divine mission. It is at this time that the individuals who will make Russia the spiritual capital of the world, have begun to incarnate. Do not miss your opportunity to serve the world. Help these children of Earth, the representatives of the new Race.

The Hail Mary:

Hail Virgin Mary, full of grace,
the Lord is with thee.
Blessed art thou amongst women,
and blessed is the fruit of thy womb,

for thou hast borne the Saviour
of our souls.

10. Now I am ready to begin the Blessing. I have come on this day to give you a part of my heart, to give Heavenly goodness to those of you who are reading my Message. I have come to give you the entire momentum of my Love, Faith, and Hope. I am asking you to do one thing: Never forget your Divine origin and your Divine mission in the midst of your everyday matters. I love you with all my heart, and I am ready to come at your first call to help those who are in need.

The Hail Mary:

Hail Virgin Mary, full of grace,
the Lord is with thee.
Blessed art thou amongst women,
and blessed is the fruit of thy womb,
for thou hast borne the Saviour
of our souls.

Glory be to the Father and to the Son, and
to the Holy Spirit and to the Divine Mother
as it was in the beginning, is now, and ever
shall be. Amen.

**In the name of the Father and of
the Mother and of the Son and of
the Holy Spirit.
Amen!**

Rosary for Russia

Together We Can Accomplish the Miracle that Awaits Russia[20]

---

[20] The Rosary is based on Mother Mary's dictation of June 23, 2011

In the name of I AM THAT I AM
Most Holy Mother of God,
beloved Mother Mary,
I pray on bended knee to you.
Words fail me to express the depth of
Love in my heart that I feel toward you.
Please accept my Love and gratitude.
You know what is most important for
the growth of my soul at present.
I am asking for your help and support.
I ask you to help me not to forget in
the midst of the hustle of the day
about those quiet minutes of our
commune which my soul remembers.
May my unbreakable bond with you
support me in my life and help me
not to forget about the Higher Path that
I intend to follow in this life.
Amen.

In the name of the Father and of the Mother
and of the Son and of the Holy Spirit.
Amen.

1. I AM Mother Mary. I have come today to talk to you again, my beloved. I have come with one thought: to strengthen you in your Service. Now the time has come for those few who remain loyal to God and to me, His faithful servant, to demonstrate their faith and devotion. The new Divine mercy has allowed the opportunity for Russia to continue. And you know that for me, it is a special country. This is the country that I have been patronizing for many hundreds of years. And now is the time when you can offer your invaluable help to the Ascended Masters through your Service. Beloved, I am asking you to take my words seriously. I wish that my words will enter into your hearts, and stay there for whole time that you are in embodiment.

The Hail Mary:

> Hail Virgin Mary, full of grace,
> the Lord is with thee.
> Blessed art thou amongst women,
> and blessed is the fruit of thy womb,
> for thou hast borne the Saviour
> of our souls.

2. So beloved, I have come with a request, and this request concerns your prayers. Your prayers are the help that you can provide now. Very few devoted and sincere hearts are incarnated now. The pressure on them is too high. However, muster up your strength. You will not have to

wait long, beloved. We are expecting the New Day to dawn over Russia, and then over the rest of the world. In recent times throughout history, I appeared to many Saints in the land of Russia. I begged them for help at those moments when storm clouds were gathering over the Russian land, before foreign invasions and threatening times. You know St. Sergius of Radonezh and St. Seraphim of Sarov, but you do not know the many hundreds of other Saints who prayed at my request and gave me the energy of their prayers for protection during hard times.

The Hail Mary:

Hail Virgin Mary, full of grace,
the Lord is with thee.
Blessed art thou amongst women,
and blessed is the fruit of thy womb,
for thou hast borne the Saviour
of our souls.

3. Now there is no longer the protection over Russia that was obtained by prayers in those glorious times when devotees of the Spirit moved to the deserts and forests to give me the energy of their prayers. When the space is not protected with prayers, then all the abomination of desolation penetrates there. You see it all around, but you do not know how to escape. You are seeking protection, and asking for protection. Beloved, the Heavens can only give you help

when it sees that you are also applying all your efforts, and devote all your free time to prayers and to prayer vigils.

The Hail Mary:

Hail Virgin Mary, full of grace,
the Lord is with thee.
Blessed art thou amongst women,
and blessed is the fruit of thy womb,
for thou hast borne the Saviour
of our souls.

4. The space over Russia needs protection. And all the Hosts of Heaven cannot protect you if there is no free will and aspiration on your part, if there is no effort applied from your side. We come at your calling and answer your prayers. But now is the time when you should answer my call. You must show your free will and diligence. There cannot be an unlimited flow of mercy from the Heavens if Heaven does not see your efforts.

The Hail Mary:

Hail Virgin Mary, full of grace,
the Lord is with thee.
Blessed art thou amongst women,
and blessed is the fruit of thy womb,
for thou hast borne the Saviour
of our souls.

5. Many people do not know what to do or how to help in this difficult situation that has formed on

the planet. I am telling you that the simplest help is in your prayers. There are no limitations and there cannot be any limits on prayer. It does not matter what religious confession you belong to. It does not matter what nationality you are. When you pray sincerely, even the words of the prayer are not important because you are elevating your consciousness to the level of the Ascended Hosts, and there a direct exchange of energy occurs between our planes of Being. Then, even the most impossible things can happen. And the miracle that the people of Russia have always hoped for, can finally take place.

The Hail Mary:

Hail Virgin Mary, full of grace,
the Lord is with thee.
Blessed art thou amongst women,
and blessed is the fruit of thy womb,
for thou hast borne the Saviour
of our souls.

6. Your land needs protection. Your planet needs protection. Each of you needs protection from the forces that are raging because their time is coming to an end. You will not have to wait long for more joyful times to come. As it was in the times long ago when the Saints prayed for my land and protected it from the hordes, prayer is also needed in your time.

The Hail Mary:

Hail Virgin Mary, full of grace,
the Lord is with thee.
Blessed art thou amongst women,
and blessed is the fruit of thy womb,
for thou hast borne the Saviour
of our souls.

7. Not many of you can devote even one hour a day to praying. And I can count on the fingers of one hand those who dedicate all their free time to praying or meditating on my image. Beloved, God grants you the opportunity. And a very small thing is needed from you: to respond to my request with your daily efforts. The power of prayer is the weapon that you can use to oppose any violence, any bloodshed, and any injustice that exists in your world.

The Hail Mary:

Hail Virgin Mary, full of grace,
the Lord is with thee.
Blessed art thou amongst women,
and blessed is the fruit of thy womb,
for thou hast borne the Saviour
of our souls.

8. There cannot be miracles that do not have the support of Heaven. And in your time, there is an opportunity for a miracle to happen. And you can foster this miracle with the efforts of

your hearts. Stay in peace and goodness. Focus all your efforts on praying for those who are unwise and enchained by ignorance. Pray for the enlightenment of your rulers. Even the utmost sinner can repent, and all his abilities and talents that he was wasting on sinful acts, he can direct at serving God.

The Hail Mary:

Hail Virgin Mary, full of grace,
the Lord is with thee.
Blessed art thou amongst women,
and blessed is the fruit of thy womb,
for thou hast borne the Saviour
of our souls.

9. Pray for the enlightenment of those people who make decisions in the fields of education and health service. Pray for the salvation of the souls of those who have lost all sense of shame, robbing the invaluable riches of my land. Sin and ignorance can be replaced in a flash by holiness and awakening. And the voice of God will stop them, as it stopped Paul in his time with the exclamation, "Is it hard for thee to kick against the pricks?" It is impossible to struggle against God. Every step that you take against God and His servants creates very heavy karma that must be worked off with suffering, blood, and sweat. The land of Russia and its people have suffered

enough. There is a bright opportunity ahead that can be manifested.

The Hail Mary:

Hail Virgin Mary, full of grace,
the Lord is with thee.
Blessed art thou amongst women,
and blessed is the fruit of thy womb,
for thou hast borne the Saviour
of our souls.

10. I ask you to replace your despair with faith and aspiration. I am asking you to find in your hearts the feeling of unconditional Love that can grant salvation to many lost souls in these hard times. I am calling you to the most elevated states of your consciousness. Pray in the language that you can, with words that you know. Aspire to me, and I will reside wherever you are praying. Together we can accomplish the miracle that awaits Russia.

The Hail Mary:

Hail Virgin Mary, full of grace,
the Lord is with thee.
Blessed art thou amongst women,
and blessed is the fruit of thy womb,
for thou hast borne the Saviour
of our souls.

Glory be to the Father and to the Son, and to the Holy Spirit and to the Divine Mother as it was in the beginning, is now, and ever shall be. Amen.

In the name of the Father and of the Mother and of the Son and of the Holy Spirit.
Amen!

I am ready to stay with you in your prayer.

I am ready to join the people who appeal to me in their heartfelt prayers and ask for help.

God gives you unprecedented opportunities. God is ready to come to every aspiring person during sincere prayer. And together with Him I will stay with each of you.

I am craving for the moment of your sincere prayer in order to come and to reinforce it.

Mother Mary, June 23, 2013

Recommendations on praying Rosaries

There is one very important point which must be recalled, and which should never be forgotten. It concerns the reminder about the constant maintenance of a reverential state of consciousness during the reading of the Rosaries, and during any spiritual work of yours.

Try to keep your thoughts concentrated on the Higher Reality. Never forget that at the moment when you read the Rosaries your communication with God takes place. And you must constantly feel reverential awe and keep in check any carnal thoughts and feelings. If you are in an irritated state after an unpleasant talk or a quarrel, postpone reading the Rosary. First, harmonize yourself by taking a walk in nature, listening to calm music or simply meditate in silence. But never engage in spiritual work in a state of irritation or imbalance.

Always remember that you color your actions with your inner state.

Therefore, start reading the Rosaries only in a harmonious state of consciousness and the more selfless your service, the more spiritual work you will be able to carry out.

Everything that you send to this world returns to you. Therefore, give generously, sparing neither yourself nor time for reading Rosaries. All the energy which you unselfishly give to God will return to you.

And everything will occur in the best way.

God loves you and always gives you an opportunity to go your way through life following the best Path.

About the Messages and the Messenger

Since ancient times the Masters of Shambala were known in the East. In various teachings people call them by different names: the Teachers of Humanity, the Ascended Masters, the Masters of Wisdom, or the Great White Brotherhood.

These Teachers have reached the next stage of evolution and continue their development in the Higher planes. These Higher Beings consider it their duty to help humanity of Earth in the development of its consciousness.

The method that the Ascended Masters have chosen to communicate with humanity is the transmission of the Messages (Dictations) that are written by the Messenger, who has a special method that ensures the perception of the Messages from the higher, etheric octaves of Light.

H.P. Blavatsky, Helena and Nicholas Roerich, Mark and Elizabeth Prophet were such people.

In 2004, the Masters gave the mantle of their Messenger to Tatyana N. MICKUSHINA. The Messages transmitted through Tatyana N. Mickushina are published in a series of books called "Words of Wisdom." Twenty-one cycles of Messages containing more than 480 Dictations have been received over the last 12 years. The Messages have been translated into 20 languages. More than 60 books have been published during this period of time.

"I did all my best in order to perform my job of receiving the Messages. But in reality, everything was done by God.

"I never knew beforehand who of the Beings of Light would come to give a Message. I also did not know what the topic of the Message would be. And I still cannot understand how this miracle of the transmission of the Messages happens. The work of the receiving of the Messages is lying on the verge of human possibilities, and we can only guess how much effort the Ascended Hosts applied to make this many years' work successful." (T.N. Mickushina)

The information contained in the Messages does not belong to any particular system of beliefs or to any specific religion.

The Masters speak about the current historical moment on planet Earth. They tell us about energy and vibrations, about the illusion of this world and about the Divine Reality, about the Higher Self of a human and about his lower bodies. They familiarize us with the new facets of the Law of Karma (the Law of causes and effects) and the Law of Reincarnation. They give us concrete recommendations on how a person can change his own consciousness, so as not to be left on the roadside of the evolutionary path.

"...When you are equipped with the knowledge of the processes taking place, it will be easier for you to orientate yourselves and to endure the chaos that exists, but will soon be replaced by the new order.

"...The duration of the transitional period depends on how your inner confidence is in the fact that there are much more joyous and better times ahead for you.

"You have to change your consciousness and change your approach to everything that is around you. For the new age will be based on entirely new principles! And if you stick to fear, to individualism, to limitations, then you will be left behind; you will fail to keep up with the train of evolution.

"For team spirit, freedom and those relation-ships that are based on friendship and love will be characteristic of the new age!

"Transformation of consciousness and thinking — that is what must be done first of all! And the sooner you can transform your consciousness, the fewer calamities and difficulties mankind will face in the near future." (Saint Germain)

"We come time after time not to reveal a new Truth, but to enable you to remember the Ancient Truth that you knew long ago but forgot, since you have plunged into materiality too much. And now the time has come to remember your Source and to return to it... This is the Truth that you learned in ancient Lemuria and Atlantis, in all the Mystery Schools of the past and the present that ever existed on Earth." (Serapis Bey)

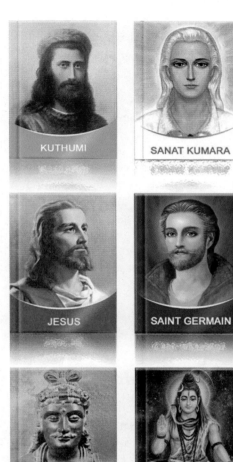
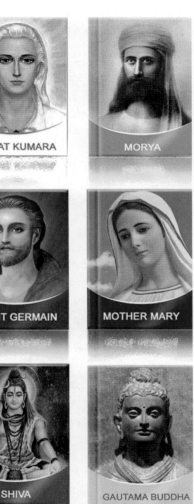

KUTHUMI

SANAT KUMARA

MORYA

JESUS

SAINT GERMAIN

MOTHER MARY

MAITREYA

SHIVA

GAUTAMA BUDDHA

BOOKS BY

TATYANA N. MICKUSHINA

MASTERS OF WISDOM SERIES

Each of the Masters of Wisdom strives to give us what they consider most vital at the present moment of transition. Every message contains the energies of different Masters who give those messages. The Masters speak about the current historical moment on planet Earth. They tell us about energy and vibrations, about the illusion of this world and about the Divine Reality, about the Higher Self of a human and about his lower bodies. They give us concrete recommendations on exactly how to change our own consciousness and continue on the evolutionary Path. It is recommended that you prepare yourself for reading every message very carefully. You have to tune to the Master who is giving the message with the help of proper music, with the help of the Master's image, or by using a prayer or a meditation before reading the message. That way you align your energies, elevate your consciousness, and the messages can benefit you.

SAINT-GERMAIN

Saint-Germain is at present an Ascended Master, the Hierarch of the New Age. In his last incarnation as the Count de Saint-Germain in the 18th century, he exerted a great influence on the course of world history. The Messages of Master Saint-Germain are charged with optimism and faith in the forthcoming Golden Age! He teaches about preparing for a New Age by transforming our consciousness, and reminds us: "Joy and Love come to you when your Faith is steadfast, when you rely in your consciousness on God and the Ascended Hosts."

SANAT KUMARA

Masters of Wisdom, first of all Sanat Kumara, remind us about our Divine origin and call us to wake up to a Higher reality, because Divine Reality by its love, wisdom, and beauty exceeds any of the most wonderful aspects of our physical world. The Messages of Sanat Kumara include Teachings on true and false messengers, Communities of the Holy Spirit, responsibility for the duties that one has taken upon him/herself before their incarnation, the right use of the money energy, the choice of everyone between the Eternal and the perishable world, overcoming the ego, the Path of Initiations, and many other topics

MORYA

Messages from the Teacher, Master Morya, have been given through Helena Blavatsky in the 19th century, Helena and Nicholas Roerich in the period around 1920-1950, and Mark and Elizabeth Clare Prophet in the 1960's. Master Morya is still actively working on the Spiritual plane to help the humanity of the World. Nowthe Masters continue their work through a Messenger from Russia, Tatyana Mickushina.

This book contains selected Messages from Master Morya. Many Teachings are given in the Messages, including the Teachings about the correct actions on the physical plane, Service to Brotherhood, the attainment of the qualities of a disciple such as devotion, persistence, aspiration, and discipline. Some aspects of the Teaching about changing of consciousness are also introduced here.

SHIVA

The present volume contains selected Messages of Lord Shiva. Many Teachings are given in these Messages; including the Teaching about God, the Teaching about Discernment of reality from illusion: which helps to ascend to a new level of consciousness and also new aspects of the Guru-chela relationship are considered.

MOTHER MARY

This book continues the Masters of Wisdom series of books. This series of books presents collections of Messages from different Masters who are most well-known to modern humanity. These Messages were transmitted through the Messenger Tatyana N. Mickushina, who has been working under the guidance of the Masters of Wisdom since 2004. Using a special method, T. N. Mickushina has received Messages from over 50 Beings of Light. Mother Mary is the Patroness of Russia. The Messages call for a review of the system of values and relationships in all spheres of life, to keep the consciousness in attunement with the Divine Reality; ways of raising the consciousness are given

JESUS

The book contains the Messages of Beloved Jesus. They give an in-depth the Teaching of Love for all Life, including to its enemies, the Teaching of Healing, the Teaching of the Inner Path, which lies in our hearts. Beloved Jesus gives knowledge of the Laws of Karma and Reincarnation, lost in modern Christianity, about the Kingdom of Heaven as a state of our consciousness.

GAUTAMA BUDDHA

The book contains the selected Messages of Gautama Buddha. Many Teachings are given in them.Here are some of the Teachings about: the change of consciousness, the current situation on the Earth, the interrelationship between cataclysms, social conflicts, wars and the level of consciousness of humanity, the Community, happiness, overcoming conflicts, discernment and Buddha consciousness. You can familiarize yourself with these and other Teachings in the Messages of the Great Teacher, given at the present stage to help people to overcome the critical situation on our planet.

KUTHUMI

This book contains Messages of Master Kuthumi. The Messages address new aspects of the Law of Karma and Reincarnation, and provide a new understanding of the structure and evolution of man and the Universe, and raise the subtle psychological moments, the knowledge of which helps us to go through life.

MAITREYA

The book contains the Messages of Lord Maitreya. They outline the Teaching about the Path of Initiations, and highlight the facets of the Teaching for beginners and those who follow the Path given in the Messages. They provide the most important elements of the current stage of the evolution of mankind: the necessity to change consciousness, liberation from ego, and establishing a connection with the Higher Self.

Author page of T. N. Mickushina on Amazon:

amazon.com/author/tatyana_mickushina

T. N. Mickushina

Mother Mary's
ROSARIES

Websites:

http://sirius-eng.net (English version)
http://sirius-ru.net (Russian version)

Books by T.N.Mickushina on amazon.com:
amazon.com/author/tatyana_mickushina

Made in the USA
Las Vegas, NV
11 April 2022

47215360R00107